AN ARCHITECT AND HIS SON

The Immigrant Journey of
Rafael Guastavino II and Rafael Guastavino III

Rafael Guastavino IV

HERITAGE BOOKS
2006

HERITAGE BOOKS

AN IMPRINT OF HERITAGE BOOKS, INC.

Books, CDs, and more—Worldwide

For our listing of thousands of titles see our website
at
www.HeritageBooks.com

Published 2006 by
HERITAGE BOOKS, INC.
Publishing Division
65 East Main Street
Westminster, Maryland 21157-5026

International Standard Book Number: 978-0-7884-4143-4

To Walter Marsh, former Headmaster of St. Paul's School,
Garden City, New York

FOREWORD
By George R. Collins

In my position as Director of "Amigos de Gaudi " in the United States, I went to Barcelona, Spain in the summer of 1962 in order to collect archival materials on Antonio Gaudi, a Spanish architect who designed a great many remarkable buildings in and around Barcelona in the latter part of the nineteenth and the first quarter of the twentieth centuries.

Gaudi frequently used the native laminated tile ceiling construction. This construction called "cohesive masonry" may or may not have originated in its present form in Spain's province of Catalonia in Medieval times but examples early became known as "Catalan" vaults. Preceding Gaudi's use it was extensively used by another architect in Barcelona, Rafael Guastavino.

The vaults of the Gothic cathedrals of Northern Europe, for example, are of fitted, wedge-shaped stones which are held together by friction and the force of gravity. Cohesive vaults are different; they are constructed of laminated tile held together by cement and thus are called cohesive masonry. In a variety of original forms they date back to Egypt, Rome and Byzantium. Used around much of the Mediterranean, they received the greatest attention in the Catalan area. The tiles are laid horizontal, in Spanish "a plano." Rafael Guastavino, complaining that there were no text books of value to him on the subject, conducted his own study on the strength and durability of this type of ceiling construction and extensively used these vaults for small spans in his work around Barcelona during the eighteen sixties and seventies. During this time he developed some engineering principles for the use of this cohesive masonry and almost alone recognized its potential for spanning greater areas.

Returning to my trip to Barcelona that summer of 1962, I was discussing with a local architect Gaudi's use of cohesive tile construction. "You should be familiar," he said, "with this type of tile work; there's a lot of it in New York City done by Guastavino.

With his engineering and good Portland cement he was able to cover much larger spans. We are proud of his success over there."

When I arrived back at my post as a professor at Columbia University and looking around, I found myself surrounded by stunning examples of this type of Catalan tile work done by the R. Guastavino Company. On the campus were the ceilings of the Columbia University chapel. Just a few blocks away was the huge Cathedral of St. John the Divine with the nave and spectacular dome supporting the floors. To name other outstanding examples, down Riverside Drive was Riverside Church, up in Fort Tryon Park the Medieval Museum "The Cloisters," down on Fifth Avenue, St. Thomas Church, and over on Park Avenue, St. Bartholomew's, all with the tile ceilings. Additionally, they had masonry acoustical tile soffits (surfaces), a type invented by the Barcelona architect's son also named Rafael. He had come with his father from Spain and had carried on the business when his father died in 1908.

In 1962 I had the good fortune to secure the entire files of the R. Guastavino Company - including the working drawings - for the Catalan Archive of Art and Architecture here at Columbia University. I found that the Company had installed their tile vaulting in more than 1,000 buildings - many of them landmarks. The invention about the time of the First World War by Mr. Guastavino Jr. (in conjunction with Prof. Wallace Sabine of Harvard University) of the sound absorbing masonry tile "Akoustolith" brought the peak amount of work during the building boom of the nineteen twenties.

In a poll taken among American architects as early as 1900 to make a selection of the ten most beautiful buildings in the United States, of those that were built in the days of the Guastavinos, all but two contained their construction. And in a selection made in 1967 by the New York chapter of the American Institute of Architects for outstanding Manhattan buildings, of those before World War II, more than half had the Guastavino tile construction.

Riverside Church interior,
from the R. Guastavino Company catalogue.

PROLOGUE

In early March 1881, a ship filled with immigrants steamed into New York bay. Ahead for those on board including a flamboyant 39 year old Spaniard and his 8 year old son was not only the surging city of New York, but a whole new world of opportunity. In the distance was the not-quite completed bridge to Brooklyn, an engineering feat now eleven years in the making and still to be proven truly safe. Off to one side was Bedloes Island. A Frenchman named Bartholdi had recently completed designs for a statue which would be erected there. In a few years she would hold up her beacon, imploring the Old World to "Give me your tired, your poor, your huddled masses yearning to breathe free..." It was a description which hardly fit the dapper Spaniard, Rafael Guastavino II. This rather fastidious gentleman and successful architect from Barcelona was carrying $40,000 in his pocket - hardly an obvious recruit for the Tammany Hall ward heelers who were in the habit of welcoming incoming ships. In his home province of Catalonia, Guastavino had developed a little-known native method for tile arch-vault construction. Only the economic and political limitations of his native land inhibited its full potential.

In America, particularly in the burgeoning, industrialized cities near the Atlantic coast, public outcry resulting from a number of disastrous fires had created a growing demand for fireproof construction – a demand that Guastavino's method readily met. More important, this turn of the century industrialization resulted in an unprecedented abundance of capital in the U.S. - enabling Guastavino to prove, with surprising economy, that great spans of masonry could be built to rival those of the ancients.

The dome of the Rotunda of the National Museum of Natural History in Washington, the tile vaults and archways of the Boston Public Library, some of the beautiful ceilings in the Biltmore Estate in North Carolina - these and hundreds of other monumental structures that will survive the proverbial thousand years are the work of this colorful, little-known Catalonian who arrived here with no knowledge of English but a heart full of ambition. His dream - to divest the wealthy and progressive country of America of its adherence to that "perishable and inferior material, wood." He ended up perfecting an ancient Mediterranean system of erecting thin masonry vaults while helping create a widespread Gothic revival in nineteenth century America.

An ancient mediterranean system.

CHAPTER ONE

INSPIRATION IN SPAIN:
OPPORTUNITY IN AMERICA

It was nearing midnight and the day's excitement was finally winding down. Rafael Guastavino V had graduated in the morning from St Andrew's, a small boarding school in Middletown, Delaware. His mother and father couldn't have been prouder. That May night, 1975, he would hear the story of his grandfather and great grandfather who made a huge contribution to American architecture, for his father had been writing a book about the family for several years, and now would share it with his oldest son.

The story begins in 1842 in Valencia, Spain when Rafael Guastavino II was born, the fourth of fourteen children of Rafael Guastavino and Pascuala Moreno. The senior Guastavino, who also had roots in Genoa, was a successful cabinet maker who gained recognition locally for carving cathedral doors. But, one of his most prized works, which belongs to a descendant in Spain is a woodcarving of the head of Christ bearing the crown of thorns.

Young Rafael's first real interest was music. He was introduced to the violin at an early age and given formal lessons; his aspiration was to become a professional musician. Although he never lost his love for music, by the time he completed his early musical training, he had fallen under the spell of the Royal Inspector of Public Works in Valencia – architect Dr. Jose Nadal, an elderly relative. Though the violin would become a great solace to Rafael later in his life, architecture now held a greater attraction. Shortly after completing grammar school, a firm of architects in Valencia hired the teenager as an office boy to run various errands. In his free time, Rafael tested his skills as a draftsman, and discovered they were considerably good. The apprenticeship strengthened his resolve to pursue a career in architecture, but it was obvious that formal schooling in the

1

subject would greatly enhance his prospects. That opportunity arose when his uncle Ramon, co-owner of a prosperous tailoring business in Barcelona, took a particular interest in him. In Spain, couples blessed with an abundance of children often find a place of welcome for some of them in the home of childless relatives. Soon, Rafael II was pleased to find himself at a new home with his uncle where he was able to attend the School of Fine Arts, which became the University of Barcelona while he was studying there.

The move to Barcelona had a significant influence on Rafael, in more ways than one. With such a large family to contend with, his father was not only limited financially but was considered to be an especially strict disciplinarian. No doubt, the adolescent Rafael appreciated the more indulgent attitude of his childless uncle. And, the city of Barcelona also provided more opportunity than did the smaller town of Valencia; his uncle Ramon's financial assistance enabled him to take advantage of it. The move also probably had a significant influence on the development of the boy's character. During his early years as a younger member of a large and still growing family in Valencia, Rafael seems to have developed the ambition and ability to sell himself and his ideas that would later come to the fore. His new situation in Barcelona, however, no doubt helped him form those traits frequently attributed to an only child; the independence of thought and initiative which would help his career and at the same time regularly complicate his personal life.

Rafael graduated from the Architectural School of the University of Barcelona in 1864. At the age of twenty two he was embarking upon his career. It was just about this time that he also decided to marry. His bride was Pilar Exposito, an orphan girl who Ramon and his wife had also taken into their home before Rafael had completed his education. Pilar's portrait as a young woman shows her to be quite fair; her long hair, arranged in two large rolled curls about her shoulders, is said to have been almost blonde, with a reddish glow.

Within two years of graduating from the University,

Rafael joined an architectural firm and won his first important commission - to design, on his own, a four story building in Barcelona. He had reached this level of professional skill in 1866, at the tender age of 24. Soon after, following several other jobs, he received commissions to design large textile mills. One of the first was in nearby Las Corts de Sierra, where a leading textile firm commissioned him to design a building that would house 64,000 spindles, 1,000 looms and 2,000 workers. The young architect was chosen because he had convinced the owners that his fresh approach to the problem of constructing a large fireproof structure was a practical one. His daring solution was to enclose the factory with a series of tile and cement vaults. Such extensive use of tile masonry was considered to be un-equaled since the time of the Romans; in fact, the technique had never before been used in this particular way.

In architecture, the materials available are always very important considerations and as lumber for building in southern Europe was always relatively expensive, it was used sparingly. Since recorded times, however, brick, tile and skilled masons to lay them have usually been plentiful, consequently all sorts of smaller openings - aquaducts, tombs, porticos, vestibules, crypts and sewers - are covered with masonry. The builder was almost always successful if he just made it heavy enough. It wasn't until the early 1800's as the Guastavino family was becoming established in Barcelona that the development of modern construction engineering first began. This amounted to a mathematical formula by load testing to accurately determine the strength and capabilities of building materials. No doubt, Rafael covered these methods in his student days. During his early career, he used the native method of vault construction - but always on a small scale. So in 1869 when he used tile vaults between beams for as huge a structure as the Battilo textile mill, it created something of a sensation.

Years later in a lecture, Rafael, related how his expand-ing the use of narrow tile vaults had been inspired by the "Cola de Caballo."

"In Barcelona, there is a family called Muntadas, considered to be a genuine representative of the aristocracy of the manufacturers of Catalonia. All the members of the family are or have been manufacturers and together they employ in the towns of Barcelona, St. Martin, Sans, Gerona and Ripoli, more than ten thousand people in their bleacheries, manufactories, dyeing and printing buildings. One member of the family owns, in the department of Zarazoza, a rich and extensive property that for centuries was possessed by the monks, and is called "Monasterio de Piedra" (The Stone Monastery). This land contains about 50,000 acres and the buildings thereon consisting of churches, convents and the palace of the abbot, of different epochs, as Romanesque, Byzantine, Renaissance and modern architecture cover about 20,000 square feet of ground. The owner, Don Frederic Muntadas (who is a great literateur and pisciculturist), lives there with his family a large part of the year. I was invited by this gentleman, through his uncles Don Jose and Don Ignacio Muntadas, to visit his property, as they intended to convert the immense convent into a summer resort.

It was October 1871, when I made my acquaintance with this estate, which is four miles from the railroad station of Alhama, Aragon, a noted hot-spring resort. It was here in that "Monasterio de Piedra" where I saw a grotto of immense grandeur, one of the most sublime and extraordinary works of nature. Imagine Trinity Church, Boston, covered by an immense natural vault supported by walls of the same nature, with gigantic stalactites of all kinds of forms and dimensions, like great chandeliers hanging from above; the floor a lake, receiving the whole light through an immense ventinel or opening like a rosette window in a cathedral, covered by the fall of the full mass of water of the river Jalon, its builder, that passes over the vault and is precipitated more than two hundred feet, taking the form in its fall of a horse's tail, which is the source of its name, "Cola de Caballo."

I had just left Barcelona after completing some buildings, among them the large manufactories of Batillo Brothers, and was under the impression that I had done something in these

4

in

buildings, inside of the Cohesive System, but within this great specimen of nature's architecture, I recognized how small and insignificant my work had been.

The thought entered my mind while in this immense room, viewing this fall of water, that all this colossal space was covered by a single piece, forming a solid mass of walls, foundation and roof, and was constructed with no centres or scaffolding and especially without the necessity of carrying pieces of heavy stone and heavy girders or heavy centres; all being made of particles set one over the other, as nature had lain them. From that time on I was convinced that we can learn a great deal from this immense book called Nature and that our ordinary system of construction is very poor, not withstanding we possessed the material for this kind of building, imitating nature. Hence, I understood why my distinguished professor of construction, Dr. Juan Torras, said one day, 'The architect of the future will construct, imitating nature, because it is the most rational, durable and economical method.'

This grotto is really a colossal specimen of cohesive construction. Why have we not built in this system?"

"Cola de Caballo" at Monasterio de Piedra, Spain.
Photo by Barbara Olmos Garcia.

5

In the middle of the nineteenth century, two discoveries proved remarkable architectural breakthroughs for Rafael: the invention of Portland cement in England, a great improvement over the older lime mortars and Plaster of Paris, and the invention of the Bessemer furnace. For the first time, steel beams, far superior to beams of iron, could be manufactured and made available in considerable quantity – and at half the former cost. With these developments, the young architect perceived that a relatively economical method for large-scale fireproof construction was finally feasible: a combination of steel, tile and Portland cement.

After the frightful fires in Hamburg in 1842, Constantinople in 1870, Chicago in 1871, and in San Francisco and Baltimore toward the end of the century, major cities were more inclined than ever to enforce new building codes calling for use of fireproof materials. To Rafael, the logical answer was to use iron or steel "I" beams, placed between brick walls and over columns, and to span the spaces between the beams with simple barrel vaults of laminated tiles laid in cement. This was the beginning of "The Cohesive Method" a building technique remarkable in its durability and virtual defiance of the laws of gravity and traditional masonry construction, for it could support not only its own weight but heavy loads above it such as another floor. Rafael started using this construction in all his building designs. When iron or steel beams were too expensive or unavailable, which was sometimes the case, he used ribs constructed of tile and cement between brick columns.

In 1872, Rafael designed and built a fine town house for himself in Barcelona at the corner of Aragon and Lauria Streets. Four stories high, it was built almost entirely of masonry, using tile for ceiling vaults. Professionally, his business was booming. In the next 8 years, he would design two woolen mills, a glass factory, a theater with a 46 foot dome, a porcelain factory, a silk mill, and two private homes. Some of his innovative designs were exhibited at the 1876 Centennial International Exposition in far-off Philadelphia, Pennsylvania. In the United States, he was awarded in absentia a Bronze Medallion.

In spite of these successful years, Rafael realized his system of tile arch construction could never reach its full potential in Spain. Many methods and building codes were antiquated and slow to change. And there were only restricted imports of iron, steel, and Portland cement. While he was in an area that was growing at as fast a pace as any in Spain, there were other places in the world which were growing faster and had better political stability, as well as greater wealth. Most of these other areas were more accustomed to using wood in volume, had more serious fires as a result, and were ripe for the introduction of a new and feasible type of fireproof construction. It was the North Atlantic coastal cities of the United States that seemed to have the best opportunities. With a rapidly growing steel industry and more available and reliable Portland cement, the vast potential for his tile-vault construction could finally be realized.

Such a realm of opportunity might well have gone unexploited had it not been for the personal problems that confronted Rafael. While his architectural career was progressing quite satisfactorily, his domestic life was not. True, he had three sons born within the first five years of his marriage. And by now the family was established in his elegant four-story town house in Barcelona with its impressive marble entrance hall and circular staircase. But, his romance with Pilar was not thriving. Rafael's passions were not limited to the field of architecture; he had developed other romantic interests.

Neither was Pilar the kind of woman who would tolerate this behavior. The illicit activity on Rafael's part culminated in a separation. Pilar left him, but the separation did not last, and within two years, a reconciliation was arranged. Pilar returned to the household and in due time a fourth son, Rafael III, was born on May 12, 1872. Even this reconciliation was short-lived. Before Rafael III reached school age, Pilar left her husband for the second and last time.

Rafael's first attempt to cope with the difficult situation was to hire a housekeeper. Rafael III could now be properly cared for. But solving that problem most certainly created others more

7

complicated, at least as far as the three older boys were concerned. For the woman Rafael hired for the job was Senora Paulina Roig, who happened to be Rafael's current mistress. All in all, it was an uneasy familial truce at Aragon and Lauria Streets. Pilar made secret visits to see her youngest son whenever her estranged husband was off at work and little Rafael was playing outside, out of Senora Roig's sight. There was yet another imminent crisis facing the Guastavino household - the oldest boy, young as he was, was approaching the age when he could be inducted into the Spanish Royal Army.

So many Spaniards had emigrated to Latin America that this possibility almost always came to mind when problems arose at home. For four hundred years the Spanish semi-feudal government had rewarded its restless gentry with land and titles in return for their conquests in the New World - a practice which had continued through the time of Napoleon and was an habitual course of action for the ambitious and restless. So, it was almost a matter of custom and instinct that led Rafael's three older boys to look toward South America in response to their current situation. They were particularly interested in Argentina, and their mother was willing, given the necessary funds, to go there.

But Rafael saw his opportunity in the United States. It would be a very rude climate for a Mediterranean native, and there was the tremendous language barrier - as yet the Northeast did not have any Spanish-speaking settlements, even in New York City. Nevertheless, Rafael settled on New York City as his destination. It was decided that his young namesake would accompany him. Whatever other reasons there might have been, the elder Rafael was loath to lose all ties with his family. The time for departure resulted in a very painful separation between Pilar and her youngest son who would always remember her furtive visits. As for Rafael's housekeeper and mistress, Senora Roig, she was quite willing to go to the United States provided her two daughters could accompany her.

Passports and other papers were granted on February 5, 1881, and the family prepared to make their separate departures.

The oldest son, Jose, preceded his mother and two younger brothers to Argentina, establishing himself in La Plata where he was to be joined by Pilar, Manuel and Ramon. Rafael's entourage, meanwhile, made its way to France and the southern port of Marseilles. There, Rafael and his son, and Senora Roig and her daughters embarked together for New York on February 26, 1881.

Rafael Guastavino II,
Courtesy of The Asheville Citizen-Times and
Citizen-times.com

NEW YORK

New York in 1881 was what it had been almost since its founding – and its indigenous traits were becoming even more accentuated entering the decade of the 1880's. New York was a vast, bustling, commercial melting pot of a port. The industrial revolution which had been pervading the North had triumphed over the slave-supported agrarian philosophy of the South. The rebels were said to have lost, but actually it was the revolutionaries in the North who had won – giving the commercial interests of the North free political license to accelerate their expansion. In New York, evidence of the revolution was burgeoning everywhere. On the waterfront, the building of the mammoth bridge to Brooklyn was the focal point of interest. Within the inner core of the city, on the island of Manhattan, the recently undertaken elevated railways with their steam locomotives were already running on no less than four elevated lines – opening the center and upper half of the island to residents who could commute to the downtown business districts. Utility poles were becoming so hung with wires that in the narrower streets, they seemed to darken the sky.

Most non-English speaking European immigrants arriving in New York could find some corner of the city in which there was a colony of their compatriots, but immigrating Spaniards, almost to a man, went to Latin America. So Rafael and his party, arriving in bone-chilling, damp New York in March, had entered a totally English-speaking world without a Spanish Harlem where they could begin to adjust.

There were many rude shocks in store for Rafael - one would come under the heading of American manners and customs. Rafael was a lover of fine wines. In Latin countries of Europe, wine is a mealtime staple, and it was one of his unhappy discoveries that so many Americans drank whiskey and rum instead. He found one American custom particularly unpleasant – the habit of chewing tobacco. Cuspidors were everywhere; tobacco juice was spat on the floor when they weren't provided, and usually round about the floor where they were. Neither was

Paulina pleased with many American customs. As there was no Italian immigration of consequence for another decade, she found it impossible to obtain any olive oil - a staple of all Spanish kitchens.

Rafael had come to a part of the New World which spoke a language foreign to him in order to sell a strange system of building - that is, seemingly unsupported ceilings and roofs, a technique that would seem dangerously fragile to people in the building industry. But he would waste no time in trying to promote his architecture. Needing an English name for his method that would describe its characteristics of structural strength depending upon tension and cohesion as opposed to mere weight, he chose "Cohesive Construction."

Rafael brought from home letters of introduction to several architects, and calls on these and others won him formal interviews. The meetings went seemingly well at first. Those he approached admired his beautiful draftsmanship, but the gentleman from Barcelona had a rather difficult time explaining himself in English. His awkward speech, delivered in an accent difficult to understand, was a substantial stumbling block. Some of the architects he visited told him that this sort of tile work might work well in Spain and Italy but would be out of place in the United States. Others simply thought him an impractical visionary. The 40-year old Rafael cut an Old World figure that was somehow both dignified and flamboyant. With his "visionary" ideas and strange accent, he made a mixed impression upon the big business scions of Victorian America. Frustrated and discouraged, Rafael decided it was time to turn to more indirect methods of attack.

It was at this point that his second "wife" left him. The members of Rafael's household, without friends, familiar sights, sounds and foods, were like a small group adrift at sea. Petty problems were exaggerated, emotions magnified. Paulina did not have such a project as conquering the entire building industry of the New World to keep her occupied, and when the thrill of entering a new environment wore off, her surroundings became merely alien, her days tedious. Favoritism, petty rivalries and a general air of friction arose in their isolated household. Paulina, with a volatile Latin temperament, had a tendency to be combative and suspicious, as well. She was hardly the pliable type, and her refusal to attempt to learn English accentuated her isolation, so that she reached the breaking point within a few months. In a huff, she packed her belongings and left with her two children for Barcelona.

It was a bleak period for Rafael, but Paulina's departure at least relieved him of the expense of a full household. He gathered his and young Rafael's belongings and moved to West 14th Street, where he had living quarters with a studio that served as his office. It was soon after moving that he got his first break.

In 1882, a new magazine called "Decorator and Furnisher" was published in New York. Rafael called on the editors, offering to make some drawings of furniture and interior decoration in the Spanish Renaissance style. The editors needed some eye-catching pages in their new magazine, so they asked him to submit some exciting sketches. Pleased with what they received, they promptly took Rafael on as a regular contributor. It was in these pages that his designs caught the eye of an architect who was on the building committee of the Progress Club of New York City. Rafael was asked to submit, in competition with some prominent New York architects, a design for their new club building, to be built at 59th Street and 4th Avenue. His design triumphed above all the rest. It was Rafael's breakthrough.

Money began flowing in as work started on the Club; and as the building's unique, brick facade took shape, it immediately began attracting attention - and not just from New York architects. Small crowds could be seen gathering on the sidewalk as pedestrians stopped to take a look. Encouraged by the turn of events and now in possession of some capital, Rafael was quick to buy several lots in upper Manhattan with a plan to build two apartment houses that would showcase the stairways and ceilings of his eye-catching architecture.

Architecture, however, was not the only thing on Rafael's mind these days. Rafael III was not quite nine years old when the family arrived in the States. He'd had several years of schooling in Barcelona, but did not speak a word of English. His father worried about sending him to whatever grade the public school might assign him to, and ending up in an oversized class where learning English would be difficult. Instead, Rafael inquired into schools with small classes, ones that perhaps used the old-fashioned one-room school house where all grades were merged. In that setting, the young boy could advance as he progressed with English.

After scouring the newspaper for advertisements, Rafael finally found a school he liked the sounds of. It was a small elementary boarding school in Connecticut located in the large home of a Mr. and Mrs. Whitlock. About a dozen boys were enrolled. On a March afternoon, Rafael and son boarded the train for South Wilton.

It was getting dark when they arrived at the station. As the sun faded and stars began to appear, the twilight was brightened by a light veil of snow on the ground. Shivering, the two walked across town to the Whitlocks' home.

It was this little school that became young Rafael's world for the next two years. While his father came to see him occasionally, it was hard for the youngster to completely shake off the feeling that he had been abandoned in what was certainly to him a strange land. The Whitlocks were kind, yet, because of his bad English, little Rafael was for a time the butt of the other boys' jokes. But being bright and hard-working, the youngster was speaking understandable English within a few months, while also starting to master his other school subjects. By his second year, the 10 year old was informally tutoring several of his school mates. But his father decided that young Rafael had progressed enough at the Whitlocks and should come home to New York to attend public school. So Rafael entered P.S. #29 in September, 1883. Now on school days after finishing his homework the boy would help out at his father's office, running errands while learning the rudiments of draftsmanship. He was taking an early interest in the business, just as his father had done at nearly the same age. He was also accompanying his father to work sites, and it was on one such occasion that the boy had an early and narrow scrape with death.

One afternoon, he and his father were visiting a large building in the city under construction. Rafael had a small contract to install a tile vault over the entrance vestibule and needed to consult with the foreman. An eight-story skeleton frame building had just been completed in Chicago, and New York was quick to copy. This particular building, in fact, was one of the tallest of its day.

Father and son located the foreman after climbing nearly to the top, the elder Rafael immediately launching into a conversation. The younger, bored with things, decided to walk down a nearby ladder, his father calling out "be careful" as he disappeared. This new "skyscraper" would one day have an elevator, but for now there was only an open shaft running down the center of the building. Workmen used it for hauling building materials up to the top floors. The hauling was done by using a rope and pulley suspended from the frame of the roof. At the other end of the rope was attached a large barrel. With time to kill and a bit of curiosity, young Rafael wandered around the quiet middle floors which were criss-crossed with boards and temporary flooring that ended at the central shaft. Up through the shaft was a slanting, smoky column of afternoon light. The workmen who had not left yet for the day were several stories above and below working on exterior walls, their voices muffled by the racket of building. Leaning out slightly and peering up the shaft to see the patch of sky at the top, little Rafael caught the dangling end of a rope to steady himself. It was just enough of a tug to tilt the huge barrel partly filled with rubble that was balanced on the edge of the shaft. For a split second, it hesitated, then the barrel slowly swung out over the drop and started down – with Rafael attached to the other end of the rope, going up. Off-balance, Rafael found himself suddenly lifted into the air, headed toward the sky and beginning to pick up speed. Swinging wildly from one side of the

15

shaft to the other, he managed at the outside of the arc to grab part of a passing floorboard – just before the end of the rope burned through the spinning pulley that dangled over the shaft. Dimly, as he scrambled onto the top floor, he heard the thud of the barrel hitting the ground eight stories below.

His father was startled to look up and see his son, pale and shaking, descending from the floor above after he had so recently seen him walking down to the floor below. After young Rafael described his adventure, the elder let loose with a tirade, which the foreman, both stunned and mildly amused, could not understand - it was all in Spanish.

Like father, like son - for more than once in the next few years, Rafael Sr. would overlook what was at the end of his own rope. Feeling settled in his New York surroundings and comfortable with the way his business was going, Rafael decided to travel to other cities to call on architects and builders. He discovered that Boston offered many opportunities for advancing his business and committed himself to a new office there, while holding on to the original one in New York - a move which added to the expenses of living in New York, owning the Manhattan lots, and paying school fees for young Rafael. Saving and investing money well was never Rafael's forte - but being on the edge of debt and ruin never seemed to bother him. In the next two years in the situation of having one large contract completed but not paid for, he discovered his savings to be at a risky level. So he made up his mind to mortgage the Manhattan lots with their partially-completed houses. It was when the potential lender undertook an inspection that Rafael discovered what he had neglected to investigate in the first place – all his tiles used in the buildings were faulty.

So work shut down immediately. Until he was paid in full for the last of the magazine drawings and his work on the Progress Club, the accomplished middle-aged architect found himself during the summer of 1883 a draftsman with a salary of $25.00 a week.

Very shortly, however, an even more serious crisis would befall Guastavino's small business: the Panic of 1884. Its effect was nearly devastating. In the widespread chain reactions of the Panic, Rafael went for months without pay for work he'd completed. And normal schedules for other building projects were delayed as well. His financial situation became so grave that he and young Rafael were forced to put up all their belongings as security at their boarding house. Snuggling in blankets which they used over end-to-end drawing boards laid out on the floor, they set up house in the office which was against all rules and regulations. They took care to time their exits and entrances to avoid any suspicion from the building attendants. In the late evenings, they took pains to appear very busy at their drawings, as other employees in the building left for home. They even did some cooking in the office, blocking the space under the door to keep the aromas from drifting out into the halls, while timing the rounds of the night watchman. One can imagine Rafael in the late evenings consoling himself with the violin, but, in fact, he never played it in his makeshift apartment. And it wasn't simply because he was sensible enough not to risk even the softest notes wafting out over the transom into the summer night. It was because he had to leave that valuable instrument with his landlady as collateral.

This was one of several panics and market fluctuations that interrupted the turn-of- the- century boom, but it was short-lived and in a matter of months, back pay, new contracts and commissions came around, and Rafael was playing his violin again. Indeed, his confidence never faltered – a characteristic that courted success on the one hand, disaster on the other, and women all along the way.

Of average height for a Spaniard in the New World, Rafael appeared relatively short and stocky and somewhat swarthy to boot. By his early forties, his graying hair had receded substantially from his forehead and temples. But his large brush of a mustache and thick sideburns, his courtly Old World manners and fastidious attire, made him an immediately attractive figure. The real source of his charm, however, was this absolute confidence which manifested in a bursting enthusiasm for his schemes in design and construction. These, he believed, would inevitably benefit the U.S. building industry. It was, no doubt, a partial result of this boundless energy that he managed to take on two affairs of the heart at just about the same time he took on two company offices.

Rafael was now a full-time commuter. With the opening of his Massachusetts office, he made the acquaintance of Miss Emma Shurr. Their friendship quickly ripened into a romance and, in time, he began living with her when in Boston, while also helping support her. And in New York that same spring he met a dark classic Spanish beauty in her twenties, a young governess of Mexican nationality named Francesca Ramirez.

Probably from the outset, Rafael's relationship with Francesca was the more romantic. She had the Latin temperament that he was so fond of. She was also ambitious. Francesca had learned to speak English while in Mexico, and with the help of a friend, managed to get money for the trip north to the U.S. Just as it was fairly common for wealthy American families to hire French governesses for their children, so there was some demand for Spanish-speaking women. By the time she and Rafael met, Francesca had held more than one job successfully.

In the next three years, Francesca became a pre-dominate figure in Rafael's life. She gave him the nickname "Pelon," which roughly translated into English becomes the intimate sobriquet "Baldy." Though Rafael continued to court Miss Shurr in Boston, it was Francesca who finally became his last, and perhaps his only true love.

After Paulina's abrupt departure from the States, and after the failure of his first marriage, Rafael felt some hesitation about becoming seriously involved. Yet despite his habit of putting work ahead of everything else, he felt a need for someone like Francesca. Deep pangs of loneliness had grown worse since Pauline left, and Pilar and his older sons had disappeared into South America. Invariably, a rogue is, at heart, a romantic. And after a year-long courtship, Francesca and Rafael decided to live together. The graying, bewhiskered "Pelon" was in his middle forties with an adolescent son. Francesca was a youthful twenty-six. The trio that moved into a house in upper Manhattan that year was introduced to the neighbors as Mr. Guastavino, his son, Rafael Junior, and his daughter, Francesca.

During the summer of 1887, Rafael decided to let his son's formal education end. Young Rafael graduated from P.S. #29, receiving a small Atlas as a reward for his "zealous application to his studies." By summer's end, the 15- year old was working full time at his father's office and was well on his way to becoming an excellent draftsman. He was spending most of his free time in the public library studying geography, history, astronomy and general books on science. But it was in the architecture section where he was most frequently found, head buried in a book.

Rafael Sr., in the meantime, secured a patent for his fireproof Cohesive Construction method. For a year or so, he had been building small sample Cohesive tile vaults of various types, and load-testing them in order to develop the needed formula to determine the capacity mathematically. Now, also, Portland cement was fully available, so there was no need to use Plaster of Paris which was prone to crack and chip. By 1888, his work was becoming widely known and was attracting the following of a number of individuals, among them a Mr. Hoffman and Mr. Bernard Levy of New York, for whom Rafael had designed beautiful homes. More importantly, Rafael was gaining the ear of many prominent architects, including one of the most prominent of all – Charles McKim of the New York office of architects McKim, Mead & White. For it was Mr. McKim's firm that was chosen to submit a design for the newly planned Boston Public Library. Rafael wasted no time in taking advantage of an opportunity, and began lobbying the firm to use his signature vaulting throughout the building for ceilings, archways and floors. He eventually would convince them that his light- weight, fireproof tiles could hold extremely heavy loads while creating beautiful curved spaces. This was a milestone in his career, for the Boston

Public Library was a large public project designed by one of the most prestigious architectural firms in the country. It literally attracted the attention of the whole building industry.

Rafael II (top right) standing on construction span of the Boston Public Library, 1889. Photo by Edward Stevens. Courtesy of the Boston Public Library, Print Department.

Builders and architectural firms were more enthusiastic about Rafael's tile arches than his business sense. With his recurring financial crises, his credit rating left something to be desired, and this was not helped by the frequency with which he overdrew his bank account. While it was inevitable that the genius of his designs and his irreproachable construction should attract a following, his business sense, or rather the lack of it, continued to make things difficult for him at the bank. He also had a tendency to grossly underestimate the cost of a job, so that many of his contracts showed no profit, and occasionally, one would show a loss.

For some time, Rafael and several colleagues were considering the possibility of forming a corporation, thinking this might result in more financial stability, and it finally transpired with the signing of the Boston Public Library contract. The company was named Guastavino Fireproof Construction Co. In addition to Rafael, the stockholders were Mssrs. Robst, Garretta, Hoffman and Levy. It was perhaps Hoffman, however, who unknowingly made the greatest contribution toward the company's eventual stability when he introduced to the Boston office a young bookkeeper named William S. Blodgett.

Tile ceiling under construction at the Boston Public Library, circa 1893. Courtesy of the Boston Public Library, Print Department.

Boston Public Library, circa 1905.
Courtesy of the Boston Public Library, Print Department.

CHAPTER TWO

BLODGETT

In June 1889, an old-school New York gentleman by the name of Hoffman drifted into the office of a friend of his in Boston. He told his friend that he had associated himself with a genius, a Spaniard, who had a new system of vault construction, that he had just secured a contract to put in some arches in the Boston Public Library and he, Hoffman, was looking for someone to take charge of this end, to keep books, tend to the bills and payrolls, etc. It so chanced that my brother-in-law Bean was in the office at the same time and was asked if he knew of any likely young fellow. He responded that his brother-in-law was looking for another job, as he was not satisfied where he was. An appointment was made for me to see Mr. Hoffman the next morning. He offered me $1,000 a year, which looked like a fortune, for I was then getting $14 per week with prospects very poor. Hoffman told me that Guastavino was a very hard man to get along with, and I would have to take my own risk.

52 × 14 = $728

I was at the office of the newly incorporated Guastavino Fireproof Construction Company on the top floor of the Pierce Building, Copley Square, early Saturday morning of June 15, 1889. At about 9 o'clock there came walking into the office a rather short, stocky man with a Panama hat, gray mustache and Burnsides whom I immediately recognized as my new boss. His salutation was something like this:

"So you are the new bookkeeper. Take this check at once to the bank and bring the money."

On my return, he made up the payroll, which, like most everything else he did of a financial character, was completely wrong. "Completely wrong," when he did not use "absolutely wrong," his favorite expression to the time of his death.

–from the memoirs of William Blodgett

It was William S. Blodgett who eventually brought order

23

to the recurring chaos of his new employer's business. Blodgett was of an old New England family with a very respectable colonial and revolutionary ancestry; but, considering that background, he had experienced a very unusual childhood. Young Will was not quite out of grammar school in 1877 when his father, after several business failures, staked himself to a trading establishment in a southern Texas town called Refugio. For four years, Refugio, Texas was literally William's stomping ground. With little opportunity for further schooling, (he claimed to be better educated than Refugio's lone teacher and probably was) William added to his skills by learning the local arts. The young Bostonian learned to ride, rope and shoot.

With superior "book education" and some free time on his hands, the teenager was chosen to serve as Clerk of Elections and bailiff for the local grand jury, culminating his career with his appointment as Deputy Sheriff of Refugio. But the boy was also now a full-fledged cowboy, as his father, from time to time, was sending him on trading missions. Like the Texan in Faulkner's The Hamlet, young William sold wild horses out of Alabama stockyards to black "cotton patch" farmers. In these cattle drives he'd move the horses 120 miles to the Texas rail head with the help of some hired Mexican "vaqueros," then live in the caboose behind the cattle cars for the four or five day rail trip.

Money was short and barter was often resorted to during these years, so the young man learned to care for the little profits he could come by. He learned well the art of complete self-reliance. But back home his mother was becoming increasingly concerned over the effect on her son of this colorful life-style. While Will was growing into a rather tall, lean, good-looking young man with a proper New England accent, when she compared him to her back-East conceptions of young manhood, he seemed in danger of becoming an uncivilized brute. It was inescapable that some of these frontier ways would rub off on what she considered a genteel, New England youth. Meanwhile, Will's two older siblings were now repaying loans their mother had made them for their college education. Will's older brother was a graduate of Brown University and already established in a

Cowboys in Refugio, Texas, circa 1880's.
Courtesy of the Refugio County Museum.

Providence law office. Mrs. Blodgett decided that it was overdue that Will, after four years in Texas, should go home to resume his formal education. So William went to live with his brother and enrolled in the local high school.

Will paid for his keep with the money borrowed from his mother and with what odd jobs he could find. Enrolling in a condensed high school curriculum, he graduated in 1884, three years after entering his first class. The next five years he would spend on several jobs. By this time, his father had returned from Texas, and his family had settled in Woburn, a small town north of Boston where his older sister was a school teacher. Will was working for the New England Machine Co., when introduced to a remarkable gentleman from Guastavino Fireproof Construction.

The meeting of Rafael Guastavino and William Blodgett brought together two men who could hardly be more opposite. One was of European background, had courtly manners, flowery accented speech, and was physically short and stocky with a dark

25

complexion and graying sideburns - the other, tall and youthful, with a broad New England accent, and aquiline features accentuated by a pair of pale blue eyes which always seemed to twinkle.

To Rafael, Blodgett was just another new young employee brought in to keep the books in Boston. On the other hand, to young Mr. Blodgett, his new employer immediately made a tremendous impression. Blodgett had been forewarned by Mr. Hoffman of Rafael's temper and high strung nature, but he felt the job was worth the risk, for Blodgett was being offered $1,000 per year, a very substantial increase in his income. Blodgett soon recognized the genius of his new employer and the opportunities he presented, and it wasn't long before he considered Rafael one of the most energetic, likeable, temperamental and interesting men he had ever met, not to mention brilliant in his profession. Blodgett's respect for Rafael soon grew into affection, as well.

The first conflict in their relationship arose shortly after young Blodgett had been hired - it was when Rafael's foreman on the big new library job failed to show up at work. Rafael was in New York, which was not unusual since he ordinarily spent less than half of his working days in Boston. Blodgett, in the absence of his new employer, took it upon himself to close the office and, in spite of his lack of knowledge of the work, went on the job to try and keep things running smoothly. Rafael arrived from New York a couple days later, and when he found the office locked went to the work site. There he found Blodgett in the foreman's position in full command, seeming to have a better handle on things than his absent foreman. Rafael guessed the foreman was drunk which later proved to be the case. But, seeing that the job was progressing so well with Blodgett, Rafael told Blodgett to stay on as foreman. Blodgett having seen several other men fired for incompetence in recent weeks told Rafael he wasn't interested in the new job. But Rafael persisted and offered him a raise. Blodgett finally agreed to accept the job only until a new foreman could be found which was accomplished within a few weeks. However, Rafael continued to increase Blodgett's salary, even after he was back at the office. Blodgett's stake in the company was rising fast.

With several other jobs in the works, another man was hired in the Boston office as a draftsman. His name was McIlvaine and he was a graduate of Columbia. The next crisis in the office would involve him and Blodgett. The episode started on a high note, however. The new Boston Public Library was going up not far from the old buildings of the Massachusetts Institute of Technology. The prominent firm of architects, McKim, Mead & White, using Rafael's "new" type of tile construction in such an important building aroused a great deal of curiosity among both MIT faculty and other leading architects in Boston. Since there was a Society of Arts connected with MIT, it wasn't long before Rafael was invited to give a lecture sponsored by the Society, explaining his new system and theories of construction. Rafael was delighted with the added interest in his work and the invitation. With great enthusiasm he began spending much of his time and that of his associates trying to get his ideas on paper in suitable English. For those helping him write the speech, the task soon seemed impossible. First, Rafael was inclined to think in Spanish, and when he tried to express these thoughts in English they often seemed to make no sense at all; and second, he was addicted to a very round-about and flowery way of expressing everything.

In the beginning, he wrote down what he could in English using Spanish words to fill in the words or phrases that he didn't know in English. Blodgett then spent evenings going over what Rafael had written and tried to put the broken English interspersed with Spanish into presentable English. All the while, concern grew over Rafael's ability to deliver the speech in his poor English. Blodgett was asked by his colleagues to approach Rafael about having someone else deliver the speech. He did so, and to everyone's surprise, Rafael agreed to a plan of having Blodgett read the speech. The text of the speech went back and forth between the two for days, as Rafael would continually make changes and additions in the margins and between the lines. Finally the day of the lecture arrived, and Blodgett took the manuscript, now full of corrections, over to the office of a typist.

She promised to have the work delivered to their office by five o'clock that afternoon. Some feeling of confidence in the prospects for the evening reappeared, but when five and then five-thirty passed and no typed manuscript appeared, there was a relapse of jittery nerves. At six thirty, the typist finally arrived and Blodgett grabbing the manuscript headed towards the lecture hall. Arriving there, he spotted Rafael and McIlvaine. Together they started to look quickly through the speech, and to their dismay realized that some of the side notes on the pages had been ignored, and also that the typist had left out some of the between line notes. And last but not least, all the equations and formulas were, without exception, missing, as typing them had evidently proven impossible. But, Rafael and Blodgett agreed the speech must go on, and Blodgett mounted the stage.

The lecture room was in the Rogers Building of the Massachusetts Institute of Technology, and upon his entrance to the platform Blodgett could recognize among the large audience many of the most prominent architects of Boston, as well as part of the faculty of the Institute, and other prominent men connected with it. The president of MIT, General Francis A. Walker, made the presentation and Blodgett began to read.

"In Cohesive Construction the components cannot be separated without destroying the integral mass. On the other hand, stone and metal structures built by the Gravity System can be at any time taken down, in the pieces out of which they were formed..."

At this early point in the speech, things began to deteriorate for Blodgett. The next paragraph had been crossed out, the following one re-arranged. Blodgett then lost his place in the maze and couldn't seem to resume. Finally, he turned to the next page and started reading again.

"... France and England like the other nations of the north have brick but not tile of the proper dimensions for the cohesive form. They are about twelve to fourteen inches long, six to eight inches wide and one to two inches thick."

As he read, Blodgett was now aware of what seemed like shadowy movements behind him, and he turned around. There was Rafael demonstrating the sizes of the tiles with his hands. He had been on the stage for some time gesturing to Blodgett's remarks. Not knowing whether to be amused or embarrassed but knowing he couldn't do anything about it, Blodgett continued and managed to get through the speech - in duet with Rafael. At the end there was good applause and both Blodgett and Rafael bowed. Many years later, Blodgett would still occasionally run into a member of that lecture audience and they would laughingly reminisce over the speech. It certainly can be said that no one in that audience would likely forget it. Eventually, Rafael had the lecture rewritten into a book and published under the title Cohesive Construction. Blodgett always claimed he could never understand any of it.

Meanwhile, the Boston Public Library was proving to be a lucrative job, and with all of the publicity accompanying its opening, the business of Guastavino Fireproof Construction Co. continued to expand. Entering the decade of the eighteen nineties, Rafael's work was flourishing. He already had an office in Chicago, as well as in New York and in Boston, and within a few years he would open ones in Minneapolis and Providence, Rhode Island. The New York office was still in Rafael's own one-story building on 57th Street near 11th Avenue, and its ceilings were of his own tile work. An advertisement in "The Architect and Building News" of June 18th, 1892 showed an illustration of the building's central tile dome under construction. Listed below the illustration were the names of over fifty buildings in which Rafael's company had installed ceilings of tile, including The Plaza Hotel and Mt. Sinai Hospital in New York City; Phillips Academy Laboratory at Andover, Massachusetts; the Morgan Stables at Newport, Rhode Island. At the St. Joseph's Seminary of Yonkers, New York, visitors gazed up at steep roofs of tile held up by tile ribs over tile ceiling vaults.

ASHEVILLE

In the late 1880's, Mr. George W. Vanderbilt, a wealthy descendant of the "Commodore," decided to build the most magnificent mansion in America - a house having 250 rooms. He chose a large tract of land near Asheville, North Carolina to build on, largely because of the agreeable climate. It was to be modeled after several of the chateaux of the Loire Valley in France. No expense was to be spared in a quest for perfection. An extraordinary feature of the mansion was to be a copy of the famous winding stairway of the Chateau at Blois. This massive stone stairway had been designed and built so that horses drawing a coach could ascend to the upper floors. Well-known architect, Richard Hunt, hired Rafael to put in beautiful, fireproof ceilings in parts of the mansion - in a vestibule, portico, a winter garden and the basement. The huge basement would eventually hold a swimming pool, gymnasium and bowling alley, in addition to several kitchens and dressing rooms.

As he began work in the mansion in the early nineteen nineties, Rafael, just as George W. Vanderbilt had before him, was finding the climate and surroundings so pleasant that he decided to build himself a house in the area. In the highland plateau between the Blue Ridge and Great Smoky Mountains, Asheville was already well known as a health resort, and was home to many hotels and sanatoriums. For in the surrounding mountains which include the highest peaks in eastern North America, the summers are not excessively hot due to the altitude, and the nights are inclined to be very cool in the valleys. The area reminded Rafael of the mountains north of his old home city of Barcelona.

A main line of the Southern Railway ran into Asheville from Washington, D.C. This meant a not too inconvenient eighteen hour overnight trip from New York. On this railroad line less than twenty miles east of Asheville is the little town of Black Mountain. Near there, Rafael found a tract of land for sale consisting of some hundreds of acres of mountainside and a cleared valley with a little stream running through it. While it was only a few miles south of Black Mountain, it was not easy to get to, since the so-called road by it was hardly more than a mountain trail. However, this accounted for a low price, and Rafael paid only a few dollars an acre for it. It was his intention to build a house of his own here some day on the edge of the valley.

In his position as bookkeeper, Blodgett had his thumb on the fiscal pulse of the Company. There it was obvious to him that in spite of the Company's apparent success, they were skating on very thin ice, mostly because of the lack of reserved capital. This worried Blodgett, for, among other things, he had become engaged to be married in 1893 and knew he would need greater financial security in the future. While his position with Rafael seemed relatively secure, he was still in no position to influence the fiscal policies of his employer, or the lack of them. Nevertheless, he decided to broach the subject. He opened the conversation by speaking of his personal plans. "Mr. Guastavino, you might be interested to know that I'm planning to get married this winter."

Rafael was surprised. "Get married! What for?" he asked. "That's the worst thing a man can do. I know. I've had experience."

"I want a wife and home of my own," answered Blodgett. "A place where I can have my meals as I want them and someone to sew buttons back on my shirt."

Rafael had met Blodgett's fiance. "That child sew buttons on a shirt?" he scoffed. The fact was that Blodgett was hardly thirty, and his intended bride ten years younger, and as Rafael said, he was speaking from experience.

"I suppose no woman could live with me," Rafael continued. "You are different. Maybe you will get along."

Rafael thought that final statement would conclude the matter but Blodgett had the Company's financial stability still on his mind. "I won't necessarily need a raise when I get married," he said, thinking to smooth the way ahead. "What really concerns me is our lack of reserve funds." He used the word "our" hoping to raise some concern in his employer's mind, and not seem selfish.

"For what should we have reserve funds - to make bankers rich?" asked Rafael. "What we need is more business. We have just started. You wait and see."

But Blodgett persisted. "Some of our contracts even show a loss. So far we have been lucky these occasional losses have been small. Suppose we lose a lot of money on a big one. Suppose we have an accident on one of the jobs."

"It's my job to be sure we don't have accidents," answered the nettled Rafael. "Anyway, we are well known now. If anything should happen, we will come back. Bad things have happened before. Now I am doing more than ever. I can always come back."

Blodgett thought to himself, "Yes, you can. You have your construction and your profession. But I want to get married. We have something good here if we can make it last, but I am only a bookkeeper and if our business goes, it will be difficult for me to find another job as good as this one. There are lots of bookkeepers." He kept these thoughts to himself, however, knowing that he might just as well.

Blodgett was married in January of 1894, and the following month the thunderbolt struck. A contractor for whom they were completing a good sized contract defaulted, and they were left with practically no hope of any payment at all for their work. They had borrowed from a bank for most of the costs of the job, and the loan was soon due. Since they realized several other jobs in process of completion would show little or no profit, there was no recourse but to declare the Guastavino Fireproof Construction Company in bankruptcy.

CHAPTER THREE

BLACK MOUNTAIN

We are surrounded by mountains and wherever we go there is nothing else to see - just mountains, with trees, streams, and rivers. There are no pavements, electric lights or gas. There are no organ grinders, nor Germans, Irish, nor Orientals; just jolly Negroes who laugh so lovely it seems as though they will swallow you up...

— letter from Francesca

With his enthusiasm for his Cohesive Construction in no way diminished by the bankruptcy of the Guastavino Construction Company, Rafael nevertheless realized he'd best let the dust of this setback settle for awhile. It was necessary to keep the New York office open and the one in Boston as well, in order to finish up remaining contracts, but Rafael saw that if he removed himself for awhile from his usual sales endeavors, he could avoid some embarrassing questions about his business abilities. Counting on a little help from short memories, it might be easier to re-establish himself after a brief leave of absence.

This plan happened to fit his personal life as well, for he still held out hope of establishing a permanent home for himself and Francesca in the mountains of western North Carolina. Young Rafael (now twenty two) and Blodgett were prepared to take over, as were two other members of the New York staff - Garretta and Robst. During the summer, while the Company was being liquidated, inquiries for some new work came in on what might be called the momentum of former successes, so preparations were made to undertake this new work on a partnership basis. Blodgett in his frugal and careful way had saved between one and two thousand dollars, and with part of what Rafael could raise by borrowing on his New York real estate, the Company continued its operation in a somewhat curtailed manner. Each partner would be personally liable for any bank loans to the extent that each had personal assets to put up as security. This slim capital prevented their undertaking any large contracts, so projects consisted mostly of small items like vestibule ceilings and stairways. They were willing to limp along for awhile, regathering their meager resources, while Rafael in North Carolina began preparing drawings for his new home.

✱✱✱✱✱✱✱✱✱✱✱✱✱✱✱✱✱✱✱✱✱✱✱✱✱✱✱✱✱

Francesca's pose as Rafael's daughter had from time to time presented problems and embarrassments. So with plans to move to Black Mountain the following year, the fall of 1894 seemed a good time for Rafael and Francesca to remedy their situation. Both were Roman Catholics and both concluded that the unsettled circumstances surrounding Rafael's former marriage might make it difficult to get married in the Roman Catholic Church. Over ten years had passed since Rafael's wife left Spain, and he didn't even know whether or not she was still living, so he and Francesca decided to place advertisements in the papers to try and gather information regarding the vanished Pilar. There was a required waiting period; but the legal deadline passed with no word from Rafael's estranged first wife. So, the two went on with their wedding plan. A license was issued for the marriage of one Rafael Guastavino, age 51, to Francesca Ramirez, age 33, of New York City, and on September 12, 1894 they took their vows in Boston. Leaving young Rafael in residence at their upper Manhattan house, Rafael and Francesca departed for Black Mountain and their honeymoon, which was to be spent beginning construction of their grandiose new home.

In his efforts to promote masonry construction, Rafael had written such statements as, "America, a wealthy and progressive country, still adheres pertinaciously to the use of that perishable and inferior material, wood." Now he was forced to swallow his words for in his present curtailed financial situation, it was simply beyond his means to proceed with plans to bring cement, brick and tile for his Cohesive Construction into Black Mountain - not to mention the skilled masons to build the house. In fact, the only reason he was able to proceed at all at this point was because of the large supply of good timber from nearby sawmills, as well as competent local carpenters, which made building a wooden house comparatively economical.

After he and Francesca moved into a Black Mountain boarding house, Rafael hired men with horses and the needed tools for clearing the site. The biggest problem for the couple was getting themselves - not to mention the workmen and the materials – into the site. For the so-called road had never been anything more than a trail through the woods, hardly wide enough for a wagon. Since some time had passed since any clearing had been done along it, wagon drivers had to watch out to keep branches from hitting them in the face and knocking them over. In a letter of October 1894, Francesca wrote the younger Rafael ...

I seldom go to the property in the morning because the roads are so bad but sometimes Pelon gets another horse for me from the livery stable and I accompany him. We have to go on horseback because of the roads. They are so bad they should not be called roads; they are just paths through the woods on mountainsides which they call roads. When I go, I have to get up to be ready by six-o'clock for breakfast, and then perform like a circus rider to go through paths which are only a foot and a half wide. You would think that if there was a fall both horse and rider would end up as hash down at the bottom of the valley.

...I wish to tell you that Pelon is worse than ever about his work. The day before yesterday he got up at three o'clock to leave and finding that it was so early he had to go back to bed. Nevertheless, he seems to get up earlier every day; this morning it was twenty minutes to one! So every morning he has to go back to bed until five o'clock. Then he gets up and dresses and goes down by himself to breakfast at six o'clock. Then off to the property to make the men lively building the house. That is the way it has been every day since we have been here – he never seems to slow down.

37

...We came to Black Mountain because it is a cheap place to live; the board here is $6.00 a week each. Our room is nicely situated near the railroad track so that all are awakened by the five o'clock freight train....

Despite all the problems, the walls went up and the roof was on the house by December. Rafael decided to halt operations for the winter and he and Francesca returned to New York to gather their possessions to take to Black Mountain come spring. Francesca concentrated on packing while Rafael worked on drawings for projects that had come into the office during his absence. Upon arriving in New York, he made some tentative calls to architects whom he felt would give him a sympathetic hearing. His strategy worked as projects came in to keep the Company going during the summer.

In March he made a quick visit to Black Mountain to hire plasterers and other workmen to finish the interior of the house, then returned to New York to make final preparations to leave their residence there. With the new house finally in livable condition, the couple forwarded their furnishings and possessions by rail freight, then left to set up housekeeping in North Carolina.

From then on, Rafael would be out of New York nearly half of the time, so Blodgett was now in charge of dealing with the banks. Not only did he have his fingers on the fiscal pulse of the company's operations, he assumed the saddle in all their financial affairs. Since Rafael was dependent on him for a significant part of the company's operating capital, he felt obliged to give him veto power over any of his own fiscal decisions. Blodgett would now carefully check Rafael's figures on estimates, and because of this Rafael used a lot more care and judgement in preparing estimates for submission to architects and builders. In short, the elder Rafael continued to call the tune when it came to design and engineering, but Blodgett did so when it came to fiscal matters. This arrangement soon became habit and Rafael was forced to confine his fiscal irresponsibility to his personal affairs.

During the course of his parents' move to Black Mountain, the younger Rafael had become very close to Blodgett. He was also finding Boston both personally and professionally agreeable. By the time his father and Francesca had settled themselves in Black Mountain, young Rafael had moved to a boarding house in Woburn. At the age of 23 he already possessed 10 years of experience at the drafting table. Having ended his formal education at 13, he had learned much on his own. With the help of an engineer who worked with his father, he had mastered graphic statics, the science that deals with stress in structures - that is, how to determine the amount of pressure masonry can withstand before it bends, breaks or cracks. Graphic statics is accomplished by a complicated system of directional lines, rather than by using mathematical formulas, and was essential for Rafael who lacked any knowledge of algebra; it would serve him well for the next 30 years. However, it was during this spring of 1895 that the young architect's skill in drafting and design was borne out by a remarkable triumph for one his age – the first of many others to follow.

For six years the Architecture League of New York had held an annual design contest called "The Annual Competition for the Medals of the Architectural League." The category for 1895 was "A Church in the Colonial Style." Rafael Jr. entered a design for a church which was very much in the regional New England style: a sharply pitched roof and tall steeple gave his entry a distinctly conservative air.

The morning mail at the Boston office contained the exciting announcement: the judges awarded his entry the winning place and the gold medal. Young Rafael could hardly wait to tell his father who at the moment was on the overnight train from Black Mountain scheduled to arrive in New York within an hour. The son decided that the triumphal news warranted a telephone call. At the time a long distance call was not only expensive, it was difficult to get a good connection. Furthermore, while the New York office had a telephone, the Boston office did not. Rafael Jr. not only had to make arrangements to use a telephone outside the office, he had to calculate the timing so that his father would have enough time to reach the New York office from the station. During the inevitable pause while he waited for the operator to get his call through, some disturbing thoughts began to penetrate his general euphoria. Since it was most unusual to use the telephone for a long distance call, Rafael thought his father would probably think some calamity had befallen them in Boston. It was an expensive indulgence, of course, the elder Rafael would no doubt think it a waste of money. In fact, Rafael Sr. disliked using the telephone at all.

So young Rafael decided quickly that he would deliver an impromptu report on their latest ongoing job in Massachusetts, in order to make the call seemingly important. The Company was in the process of installing the basement ceilings of a small new bank in Boston – ceilings that were designed to carry the load of the first floor. The Company had never done any previous work for this particular architect, and the man had been apprehensive about the strength of the vaults – feeling that some steel tie rods across the top of the vaults under the floor might be necessary to hold the thrust. The senior Rafael, however, maintained that these tie rods were completely unnecessary since the vaults were at ground level; the containing exterior walls would have solid backing as well as the added solidifying weight of the whole building above. Now that the job was far enough along that the centering (temporary, wooden supports) had been removed from the first vaults and no cracks had appeared, the architect was reassured and, in fact, quite pleased.

In his New York office, Rafael just arrived and was sitting at his desk going over the mail when the telephone rang. He remained absorbed in his mail while Robst answered the phone. "Yes, yes," Robst said a number of times before turning to Rafael to tell him, "It's Boston. It's your son in Boston. He wants to speak to you."

Now Rafael was both surprised and alarmed. "What's happened," he asked himself. "An accident?" He was sure the Boston bank couldn't have collapsed – but one could never know about a new job. "Allo, Allo," he said as he put the receiver to his

SEVENTH ANNUAL COMPETITION FOR THE MEDALS OF THE ARCHITECTURAL LEAGUE.
A VILLAGE CHURCH IN THE COLONIAL STYLE.
GOLD MEDAL AWARDED TO RAPHAEL GUASTAVINO, JR., BOSTON, MASS.

41

ear. There was a dim voice over the wires.

"This is Rafael in Boston," said his son, unnecessarily.

"What's the matter!" said the elder in a loud voice.

"Nothing," Rafael Jr. hastened to answer. "We took out some centering at the bank job yesterday morning. It's all right. Mr. Abernathy came to have a look yesterday afternoon and he's very pleased. He doesn't seem worried now at all."

"I know, I know," answered Rafael. "He never had any reason to worry. But why do you telephone from Boston to tell me that?"

"There's something else I want to tell you," Rafael Jr. answered. "Do you remember the sketches of the church you saw me working on when you got back from North Carolina last spring? Well, I won. I won the competition."

Rafael, who had forgotten all about the competition since he had taken little interest in it in the first place, said, "Good, good. You got us a new job. A church you say? How big is it?"

Rafael Jr. was alarmed at the turn the conversation had taken. "It's not a new job. It was for a contest – the Architectural League Contest – I won the gold medal."

"Oh!" answered his father. "I see. A gold medal you say? Well, that's good. That's good. Is there anything more you want to say?

"No..." answered his son.

"Well, I will say goodbye then. A call like this is very expensive. Goodbye." He hung up the receiver, returned to his desk, and picked up another letter. "The Architectural League," he muttered. Rafael thought to himself, and then paused a moment, musing, "Yes, now I remember the announcement of the competition – the competition for the medals of the Architectural League. So Rafael really won the gold medal? There must have been some very good entries, too. Of course," he tugged on his moustache, "prominent architects don't enter – but their best draftsmen sometimes do, and often the draftsmen are better architects than their employers. Prominent architects are good salesmen, that's all. The draftsmen they employ are often the best architects. I did well when I taught Rafael." A feeling of pride settled over him as he resumed his perusal of the mail – now with a smile on his face. "I'll have to remember to congratulate him when I write to Boston."

Back in Boston, however, Rafael Jr. left the telephone feeling suddenly quite dejected after the hours of elation that had buoyed him since he received the announcement in the morning's mail. But he told himself that whether it seemed that way or not, his father must be pleased. There was no one else who could understand; Blodgett, immersed in all his figures, just couldn't. And Rafael did so want to please his father.

This sort of minor setback, however, never weakened his determination. Young Rafael had been and was still inclined to be an "all work and no play" young man. Already, by his mid-twenties, his dark wavy hair was becoming streaked with gray. Of medium height like his father, in other respects he took after Pilar. While the elder Rafael was not particularly dark for a Spaniard, he appeared swarthy in contrast to most Americans. Rafael Jr., on the other hand, took after his mother with his pale complexion and pale blue eyes. In the Company, he was already beginning to assume a more formidable position; as the volume of business picked up, his developing talents were becoming more important and were being put to good use. During the extended absences of his father in Black Mountain, he was well able to carry on much of his father's efforts.

With Rafael Jr. and Blodgett handling the day-to-day work at the office, the affairs of the old company were soon wound up. By 1896 the office rent and overhead had been assumed by the partnership, and again new business was on the rise. Modest but steady profits were adding up, and within the year their financial position was substantially improved. With this welcome turn of events, they began to look about for larger contracts - among those being negotiated by the elder Rafael was the projected Munsey Building in New London, Connecticut. Blodgett, with a widening circle of influence in the building industry around Boston, was also beginning to have some success on his own. His increasing capabilities in promoting the use of Cohesive Construction had played no small part in the Company's comeback. In addition to the Muncey Building contract won by Rafael, Blodgett contracted two other comparatively large jobs: one, the American Soda Fountain Building, and the other, the American Type Founders Building, both in Boston. These projects were quite profitable, so in 1897 a new Company was founded with Rafael Sr. taking a little more than two thirds of the stock and Blodgett taking a good part of the rest. Rafael Sr. filled the President's chair and Blodgett took the post of Treasurer. While young Rafael had only a small capital interest in the corporation, his growing importance in the Company won him the third directorship and the post of Vice President of the R. Guastavino Company.

By 1898, Rafael Jr. was in charge of a number of out-of-town jobs, including the new Cohesive tile dome for the library at The University of Virginia, designed by family friend, Stanford White. The dome replaced the original wooden one done by Thomas Jefferson which had been destroyed by fire a few years before. But about this time serious problems with tile manufacturers arose that slowed work to a near standstill. The trouble involved controlling kiln temperatures which affected the color and quality of glazed tile. Whenever the Guastavino Company ordered tiles from the manufacturer's samples, the orders needed to be filled to match the original and this was no easy task. There were many rejects before the order could be filled exactly right and then shipped. Larger orders might have led to better results, but most jobs were small, and a number of buildings required tiles in several different colors. Getting ones that met just the right specifications, and were sent in time to finish the job was a constant problem.

Rafael Jr. knew that his father was very familiar with the principles of tile manufacturing, since his native province in Spain abounded with small tile factories and since his early work led to many factory visits. Young Rafael tired of hearing complaints from builders and architects over delivery delays and lack of uniformity in his tiles, was eager to try out an experiment. So, in the late winter of 1898, with building operations at their normal slowdown, he set off for Black Mountain where, with the help of his father, he planned to experiment with building his own kiln.

CHAPTER FOUR

Books

"RHODODENDRON"

By the turn of the century, Rafael found his father comfortably settled at Black Mountain in what family members called "Rhododendron" and townspeople had nicknamed "The Spanish Castle." In his sixties, with many years of hard work behind him, Rafael Sr. was leaving most of the management of the business in the capable hands of his son in New York and Blodgett in Boston. He would still go occasionally to New York but much less since his friend and colleague Stanford White had died. Rafael was actually on a trip to New York when the startling news broke. White had become embroiled with a wealthy Pittsburgh man, Harry Thaw, over the affections of Thaw's wife, showgirl Evelyn Nesbit. While White was attending an event at Madison Square Garden (a building he designed), Thaw shot and killed him. Thaw, who had gained the reputation as a Pittsburgh playboy, would later be judged insane.

Rafael would not return to New York for a long time afterwards, for in North Carolina he was content and absorbed in free time. He began to write - mostly about his opinions on architecture. Deciding to add more ideas to his book <u>Cohesive Construction</u>, which was based on his Boston lecture, he wrote <u>The Functions of Masonry</u>. More familiar now with the English language, he wrote it without the benefit of Blodgett's revision.

He was also able now to indulge himself to his heart's content in music. He began playing the violin again, and tried his hand at composing when the spirit moved him. He found time to begin and polish some shorter compositions which he'd begun in earlier years, and commence work on new ones. Among those he finished were some lively waltzes.

As for running the farm, Rafael found a project, which, while not very profitable considering the skill and attention it required, nevertheless gave him a lot of satisfaction and some

Rhododendron (a.k.a. The Spanish Castle),
Courtesy of Christmount Christian Assembly.

income. Finding it hard to market the crop from his maturing apple trees, he decided to crush part of the apples for cider. Then, not content with doing something as simple as selling the cider or fermenting it for distillation, he tried bottling and corking it at the proper moment during fermentation, making what he called "champagne cider." With a little promotion, his cider was very saleable. The bottles were small, the price quite low, and he succeeded at selling many full and half cases of it.

Rafael also loved making wines from his home-grown grapes. In order to promote the aging of his wines under the right conditions, he built a wine cellar in the side of a hill in the most convenient place he could find. It happened to be alongside his entrance lane near the main gate to the house. Rafael took great pride in his wines, and any dinner guest at Rhododendron was persuaded to render an opinion on the different types and vintages. It was not unusual for a lucky or unlucky guest, depending on the viewpoint, to leave in a rather tipsy condition. One gentleman years later recalled visiting Rhododendron to take photographs of a Sunday school picnic, and ending up stumbling home after sampling too many of Rafael's wines.

Rhododendron was continually in a state of growth, for as surrounding land became available, Rafael would buy it up. The farm now consisted of about 1,000 acres. And in the midst of it, the large 3 story house with its wooden tower, tall chimney and rustic chapel displayed a unique brand of Guastavino architecture.

Rafael loved being with Francesca although their relationship was not always the smoothest. Two such strong Latin temperaments would occasionally clash, but on the whole their strong attachment for each other predominated. Francesca did have a habit which was somewhat annoying to Rafael, though he tried to hide it. That was, whenever he would go on a trip, she would hire a carpenter and have him build something small on the place to please her husband on his return. There was the summer house by the pond, and, on another occasion, a shelter near the gate. But these surprises were somewhat irritating to him, for the expert likes to design his own buildings, however insignificant.

Summer house at Rhododendron,
Courtesy of Christmount Christian Assembly.

About this time, Rafael was back in touch with several members of his family in Spain. Two of his brothers were now in religious orders, one a chaplain in the Spanish Army, and the other, Antonio, having been left a widower, became a Franciscan monk. Prior to the Spanish American war, Antonio had been an organist at the Havana Cathedral. Both brothers owned a sheep ranch together in Puerto Rico, but with the withdrawal of Spain from the West Indies, they returned home to Spain. It had been more than 20 years since Rafael had seen them and he started to plan a reunion.

Also, at this time, he was in touch with his three sons in

Argentina finding that the eldest, Jose, was now a successful architect in Buenos Aires. His youngest son, Ramon, had moved to Mendoza in the West, entering the wine business, while Manuel had become a building contractor. The following is part of a letter (translated) from Manuel:

Buenos Aires, November 23, 1905

Dear Father:

.....Once again I am obliged to appeal to you for new facts which are of great interest and urgency. It concerns the following: nowadays here in Buenos Aires, there is an enormous amount of construction going on and above all, of buildings that are quite high so that it is necessary to have mechanical aids to facilitate the lifting of materials during the construction of the works. This very day I have submitted plans and a sheet of conditions as a bid for work that will be around a million pesos and that is about 33.00 meters high on top of a terrace, plus a tower with other supports that form a total of 43 meters in elevation. Naturally, we need, in case our bid is accepted, one or two elevators, steam or electric, like the ones they use in New York. Here, they already have them, but they are under the control of firms that ask three times what they are worth. As I suppose that in New York now the system is more generalized and that there exist several manufacturers, it will be possible for me to obtain them cheaper ordering them from New York directly from the factory...
.....Without anything further for now, greetings from all to you and to Rafael and from me, too.

Your affectionate son,
Manuel Guastavino

It is unknown whether Rafael was able to help ship any elevators to his son.

There is evidence that around this time Rafael discovered that Pilar had died, and this affected the rest of his life - personally and professionally. The way was now open for a rapprochement with the Church, the first step being that he and Francesca become members of the Roman Catholic Church of St. Lawrence in Asheville. From then on, they set aside a room in the house in Black Mountain as a chapel where Mass was said; here they would repeat their marriage vows. Also, they began to gather large stones during the slack farming season, and when there were enough for a sled load, a team of horses pulled the heavy sled up the mountain behind the house to a site with a beautiful view. The intention was to build a chapel there when enough stones were collected.

By 1906, the wooden church built in 1888 for the parish of St. Lawrence was fast approaching the point where it was too small for the number of Catholics in the growing city of Asheville. Rafael learned this first-hand when one Sunday he and Francesca arrived at the Church and were unable to find seats. Father Peter Marion was the pastor of St. Lawrence and he and Rafael were developing a friendship as his Church was occasionally using the chapel at Rhododendron. It was inevitable that the subject of a new church for the Asheville parish should come up - and that Rafael would offer to draw up plans for it. Rafael prepared some sketches and, as expected, he suggested that the church edifice be built of masonry with a generous use of Cohesive Construction. He wanted it built in the Spanish Renaissance style so familiar in Latin America. With its twin towers with small domes atop each tower, it would be recognized as Spanish Colonial. In this new St. Lawrence Church, the crowning feature was to be a large elliptical dome of Cohesive tile, very unique for a church in the United States.

Rafael offered to donate all the Cohesive construction and by 1907 was at work on a complete set of detailed drawings. Masons from around the area came to Asheville to start work on the outer walls and the roof which consisted mainly of the elliptical dome. For a description of the church, and a revelation of the untimely death of Rafael Sr., there are three paragraphs from a booklet about the church printed several decades after it was built.

"The style of the church is Spanish Renaissance, a peculiarly

happy choice since St. Lawrence was born in Huesca, Spain which is also the native land of Mr. Guastavino. The main facade has as its central figure the statue of St. Lawrence .... and over the main entrance is a representation of Christ giving Peter the keys.

One is impressed by the massiveness of the stone foundations and by the solidity of the superstructure of soft-toned brick, and one begins to see how the architect has planned to make the building, as far as any work of man can be, everlasting: there is not a beam of wood or even steel in the whole edifice; all walls, floors, and vaulting are of tile or other masonry materials, and the roof itself is of tile with a copper covering.

Entering the vestibule, which is separated from the church proper by the screens of embossed leather and of stained glass, we may pause to note again the solidity of the structure, for the very steps to the organ are without wood or nails. It is only after we have entered the church and are standing at the foot of the main aisle that we realize the beauty of the ellipse and the wonder of the dome, Mr. Guastavino's masterpiece; it is built wholly of tile and is entirely self-supporting, having a span of 58 x 82 feet, and being the largest dome of elliptical type over any church in this country. It was wholly donated by Mr. Guastavino and erected under his daily supervision; and it had not long been completed when he was suddenly stricken with an illness which proved fatal... He left the designs and plans for the Main Altar and Lady Chapel still to be made; but fortunately for Asheville and St. Lawrence Church, he also left a son, Rafael Guastavino Jr., who inherits his father's skill and generosity as well; and this son has most beautifully completed his father's unfinished work."

It had been late January when the elder Rafael was stricken with a chill; lung congestion was followed by kidney complications, and he died on February 1, 1908. Francesca was desolate. It is said that at the time of his death she had the big clock in the tower above the house stopped. She would never allow it to run again; it was a symbol that, for her, time had stopped.

Funeral services were held in the unfinished church, with many of the furnishings only temporary. Some of the music on which Rafael was at work composing was of a religious nature, including an unfinished Mass which was performed at the funeral. Befitting its hero, Rafael's body was laid to rest in a crypt especially built inside St. Lawrence.

St. Lawrence Church, Asheville, North Carolina.
Courtesy of North Carolina Collection, Pack Memorial Library,
Asheville, North Carolina

AERIAL VIEW OF CHURCH AND PARISH HALL

St. Lawrence Church, Asheville, North Carolina.
Courtesy of North Carolina Collection, Pack Memorial Library,
Asheville, North Carolina

PART TWO

Rafael Guastavino III

CHAPTER FIVE

NEW YORK

In 1908, the great Cathedral of St. John the Divine, located in upper Manhattan, was projected to have one of the largest domes in the world - comparable to the ancient Roman Pantheon's 142-foot dome. This new one would be nearly the same size as the dome over St. Peter's in Rome, and that of the Cathedral in Florence. St John the Divine was now sixteen years in the building process, and a lack of funds was the explanation for only sporadic work at the site. Some walls and roofs were in place, and four great stone arches on four huge stone piers formed the place of the projected dome crossing.

All masonry arch work of any size is generally built with interior supports called centering, and when the work is finished the centering is removed. Centering is expensive to erect, but considering the durability of the finished arch work, it is generally worthwhile. Rafael Jr. dared to consider building this tremendous dome minimizing the centering and scaffolding on which the men would work. A small amount of centering where tile was actually being laid and sufficient scaffolding for the workers was necessary, but Rafael's daring scheme employed only a small rig which would be moved along in a circular direction as the men progressed. In this way, the building of a tremendous forest of expensive centering from floor to the work over a hundred feet above could be avoided. Only then could the dome be built with the funds available.

In order to build the dome as economically as possible, Rafael's scheme was to use freshly set layers of tiles that were less than a foot thick at most. He reverted to using Plaster of Paris on the first layer of cement, which, while not as strong as the Portland variety would set firmly in a matter of hours. The use of Portland cement for the remaining layers would then provide sufficient early strength. Rafael had built smaller domes, but in mastering graphic statics, believed himself now able to solve the

59

problem of stress in any sized dome.

There is a good deal of camaraderie among crews in the building trades. It is said that when the dome was started, there were bets made among members of other crews working at the site giving better than even odds that there would be a fatal collapse while the work was in progress. Many experts with years of experience in the building industry were inclined to agree, for the rising dome of freshly laid tile with cement not thoroughly hardened would not only have to support itself and its minimal centering, but the workmen with added loads of fresh material for each day's work.

For the men commencing the work atop the great stone arches of St. John the Divine, there was yet another concern - persistent March winds. Carpenters used to working near the ground or within walls, carrying planks for the meager centering and scaffolding, found themselves at exposed heights in danger of being carried off into space by the sweep of unimpeded gusts. Nevertheless, the work progressed. Tile after tile was laid and the circle of working masons shortened as the great dome rose towards its apex, slowly enclosing the gaping space. By mid-July, the dome was well over half completed and those in charge were confident and happy that the skeptics were being proven wrong.

In the midst of Rafael's work on St. John the Divine, a developing crisis took shape in his personal life. It came about while he was visiting Denver supervising the installation of a particularly demanding contract. He became very ill. The brick-layers were working a nine hour day and the conscientious Rafael was not only on the job with the men in the morning, but long after they left. And he would often return again in the evening after dinner - checking measurements, quantities of materials and the strength of scaffolding. Dwelling in his mind, though, was the memory of an accident the year before which had frightened him. Too much tile had been laid in one day for a high rise Gothic vault. At quitting time, the whole mass of heavy wet cement collapsed and slid down the centering. Fortunately, no one was hurt, but the episode haunted him.

Arch under construction, Cathedral of St. John the Divine,
Print by Antoinette B. Hervey.
Collection of The New-York Historical Society.

Cathedral of St. John the Divine, 1917.
Print by Antoinette B. Hervey.
Collection of The New-York Historical Society.

Guastavino roof construction,
Cathedral of St. John the Divine, 1908.
Print by Antoinette B. Hervey.
Collection of The New-York Historical Society

One morning after an evening on the job and a rather restless night, Rafael could hardly get out of bed and couldn't eat any breakfast. He sent for his head carpenter, explained the situation to him and after going over with him what was to be installed that day, stayed in bed to recover from what he thought was a bad case of indigestion. The next day he felt better and was back on the job. But when the whole sequence was repeated two days later, he became upset and called in a doctor. The doctor could find nothing in particular wrong, and after questioning Rafael at length about his eating and other habits, came to the conclusion that it was "nervous prostration" - a simple case of too much work. The doctor's unusual prescription was: "Go out to the theater in the evening and enjoy yourself, or at least read a good book and get your mind off your work for awhile." While it cannot be said that Rafael immediately embraced a life of wine, women and song, he was sufficiently impressed with his illness and the doctor's advice to get involved in some relaxing pursuits.

For one thing, to make life easier when back in New York, he became a boarder in a house on Green Street in Brooklyn - a place he would soon consider home. Rafael was fond of the owner and his wife, William and Genevieve Seidel, and their children, Elsie and Henry, who were now entering adulthood.

What Rafael didn't realize was that the circumstances in the Seidel home were under the darkening shadow of declining finances. Mr. Seidel's business ventures, in contrast to those of Rafael, seemed to be continually unsuccessful, and to wash away his troubles, Mr. Seidel was starting to drink heavily. The drinking episodes led to more than one tearful session between Genevieve and her mother- in- law, who was a frequent visitor from her home in Wilmington. Genevieve had another problem as well. She was suffering from terrible headaches which were becoming more numerous and severe.

As the situation worsened, Mr. Seidel started resenting Rafael, not only because of his financial success, but also because of Genevieve. The Seidel's daughter, Elsie, was also painfully aware of what seemed like a too close and sympathetic friendship between Rafael and her mother. On occasion in the late afternoon, while working with her school books, Elsie would see Rafael come in from work, then disappear into the kitchen where her mother could be heard making preparations for dinner. Normal kitchen noises would then cease; Elsie was very conscious of the ensuing lengthy silence.

Rafael had always deplored the affairs of his father in his relations with the opposite sex - for one thing, it had led to an unhappy home life for much of his childhood. But for all his father's philandering, his father never became entangled with a married woman. Young Rafael was now more involved in the Seidel household than he realized. The lonesome young bachelor was becoming part of what can be best described as a platonic "menage a trois."

The crisis began to boil over in the late winter of 1909. Genevieve, with her increasing headaches and heavy medications seemed hardly able to cope with her household duties. Genevieve's older sister, Florence, was also living in Brooklyn and married to a very successful architect, Holland Anthony. Florence was aware of the long declining finances of her sister's household, and disgusted with her brother-in-law's financial shortcomings and his drinking. She called on her sister one afternoon and found her distraught, suffering from a terrible headache. After a long tearful conversation with her sister, Florence decided to write Mr. Seidel a note and tell him that it would be best for all concerned if he moved out of the house until Genevieve's health improved.

The letter which Mr. Seidel received was the trigger that set in motion events that no one could have foretold at the time. Needless to say, Mr. Seidel was not at all happy in his own home, and this epistle was all he needed to move him to pack a suitcase and leave. The Williams family, with whom the Seidels had summered during the nineties at their boarding house in the mountains, now owned a boarding house in upper Manhattan, and that was where he went.

By this time, it was well into spring. Since it was obvious that Genevieve would benefit from a change in scenery, she went to Bryn Mawr near Philadelphia for a visit with her mother and oldest sister. Elsie was nearing the end of the school year and about to graduate from a course in teaching kindergarten. Torn by this split in her family and still feeling much loyalty to her father, she went to the Williams leaving her young brother, Henry, and Rafael to themselves in the Brooklyn house. Now it so happened that the Williams had a young cousin who was a lawyer and had recently moved to New York seeking a more lucrative practice. The young man met Mr. Seidel at the Williams' house and greeted him by saying something to the effect of, "With the circumstances at your home, it sounds as though you have grounds for a real complaint." One remark led to another, and it wasn't long before Rafael found himself faced with a lawsuit of $50,000 for "alienation of affections."

Elsie was shocked with this latest development as much as anyone and immediately upon her college graduation in June left New York and joined her mother in Atlantic City. With the lawsuit filed but nowhere near court action, Rafael and Henry in the Brooklyn house, Mr. Seidel at the Williams, and Elsie and her mother in Atlantic City, the whole situation could simmer down a bit. But Elsie, feeling really crushed by the disgrace of it all, was determined to help find a way to resolve differences and save the family. One night after going to bed in her hotel room in Atlantic City, she lay awake thinking about the lawsuit. She was entirely free, she thought, and would be twenty-one in August. Rafael was a bachelor, also as far as she knew entirely free, and apparently lonesome. And there was no question that they were fond of each other..... alas, why not she and Rafael get married. This was the fitting piece of the puzzle that could solve everything. The lawsuit would have the rug pulled out from under it, the lonesome and successful bachelor would have a wife. Elsie could provide some security for her parents in their old age. There was even a business opportunity for Henry. It all fit so beautifully. Elsie drifted off to sleep with dreams of being known one day as Mrs. Guastavino.

The next day, Elsie thought out a plan. She would

approach Rafael in New York and, while apologizing for her father's behavior, plant the idea that, perhaps, the two of them could become involved. On the train back to Brooklyn, she mulled over how to drop the hint of her interest, and upon arriving that evening, went over to the house to see him. Telling Rafael of her sympathy for his plight, she went on to suggest they spend more time together.

For Rafael who'd always thought of Elsie as more of a niece than a potential girl friend, her new found feelings towards him would come as a complete surprise, yet a pleasant one, as he had always found her interesting and attractive. Nevertheless, he would take some time to think things through.

Working that fall in his office in Boston, he would send her cards and letters filling her in on his activities and thoughts. He, too, wanted the lawsuit settled, the sooner the better, but denied to himself that any feelings towards her related to that. Upon returning to New York, he started calling on her and was quick to give in to her charms. On Sundays they would stroll together through Prospect Park - and in the evenings settle into candlelight dinners at Delmonico's. Rafael, now finally following doctor's orders, was frequenting the theater, sharing a box with Elsie and several friends. It wasn't long before their conversation led to the subject of an engagement.

They chose to first break the news to Elsie's best friend, Helen, but Elsie was sad to find that her friend was not at all enthusiastic on hearing of the engagement. It was the difference in religion that seemed to produce a problem - but Elsie was to prove this easily surmountable. She was Episcopalian, but not against the idea of becoming Catholic and being baptized in that faith. She would go to Bryn Mawr, she thought, and stay with her Aunt Willie. There she could prepare for baptism in the Catholic Church. She then wrote her mother a note with the news of Rafael's proposal and her acceptance, and said she'd write again as soon as she heard news of the end of the lawsuit which would surely soon follow. The greatest problem was how to tell her father. How would he respond? Elsie tried unsuccessfully for several days to reach him, but it was a good friend of hers who ran into Mr. Seidel and felt obliged to break the news. As told to Elsie, her father seemed astounded, then totally dejected. His reaction would dispel any doubts about his motives, for he obviously had no Machiavellian scheme to engineer his daughter into an unlikely marriage.

The lawsuit was soon withdrawn, and Rafael and Elsie were married in Philadelphia. The two took off to Atlantic City for a honeymoon. But Rafael distracted by thoughts of finishing the cathedral dome cut his honeymoon short. By early August, he and Elsie were back in New York where they found the dome almost closed in. In a short time, he would take her up to the top to see the magnificent view of surrounding Manhattan. At the apex of the dome, she could also see the floor of the cathedral far below by looking through a tiny peep hole in the few inches of tile and cement which was all that was holding up the two of them.

Elsie's home in Brooklyn was now vacant, and Rafael decided to buy it for them to live in for the time being. There would soon be three in the Guastavino family as Elsie learned she was going to have a child the following summer. Rafael's business was booming since the completion of the dome and the surrounding publicity, and with some free time on his hands, thanks to the usual slack winter season, he started making plans to take a trip with Elsie to Mexico. For some time he had wanted to study and photograph many of the masonry domes that were built there over several centuries, some of them so old they pre-dated the arrival of the Pilgrims.

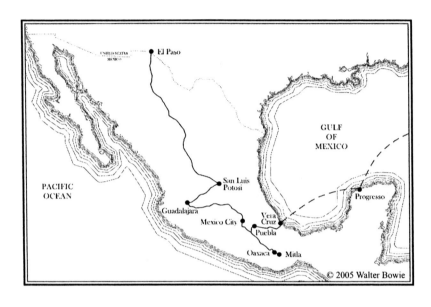

Rafael and Elsie tour Mexico.

MEXICO

In January, Rafael and Elsie left on a ship from New York destined for Veracruz with a stop over in Havana. There, Rafael, in addition to taking Elsie sightseeing, bought her some fine French jewelry. The prospect of a supply of new clothes would have been more to Elsie's liking, but Rafael felt that the lasting value of jewelry was a more practical investment. Moving westward the ship made a stop at the Yucatan port of Progresso, then went on to Veracruz. In this busy city and railroad center, they boarded a train taking them up into the central plateau region of south- central Mexico to Puebla, one of the country's oldest Spanish settlements and famous for its 320 foot high Doric cathedral. Thought of as one of the finest examples of ecclesiastical architecture in all of Latin America, the Cathedral was built during the span of a hundred years from the mid-sixteenth to the mid-seventeenth century. It was of great interest to Rafael for its huge dome and colorful tile work. Though at first feeling a little dizzy at 7,500 feet above sea level, Rafael set out to explore the Cathedral, as well as several other Spanish colonial buildings in the city including an outstanding theater and an immense bull ring. Elsie also felt the effects of the change to the high altitude, the whole time feeling, as she described it, light headed.

From Puebla, the journey continued south to Oaxaca, then by horse drawn coach accompanied by a boy outrider, to Mitla. There Rafael and Elsie stayed at a hotel that housed not only guests but the general store and post office as well. The hotel was built in the form of a square surrounding a courtyard. Since earthquakes frequently shook the area, the courtyard was often a sought-after place for guests. When warning tremors were felt during the evening, visitors would have their beds carried out into the courtyard for safety. While Rafael and Elsie didn't feel tremors sufficiently strong to frighten them, an experience on a moonlight evening certainly did. The remains of a pre-Colombian temple were considered the outstanding tourist attraction of the area, and they were persuaded by a local guide that the best time to see this temple was by moonlight. They were becoming accustomed to carrying their valuables with them, as safe a solution as any in this area which seemed quite primitive. So, on this night-time expedition, Rafael carried his money and Elsie her jewelry in packets inside their clothing. On nearing the temple, their guide announced he was to meet a man there. Then, to make matters worse for the already nervous couple, on arriving at the temple their guide led them to a low opening in a wall and announced this was the entrance. The opening was so low they had to get down on their hands and knees to get into it, and then feeling like lambs going to slaughter, they crawled through the short tunnel and across a roofless area surrounded by the ancient walls. There stood a man in the bright moonlight just like one of the high priests of ancient times who actually waited in this very temple for the human sacrifices to begin. The man greeted them all and then passed over to their guide, his employer, the receipts of his day's work as attendant at the temple. Elated with relief at being safe, Elsie and Rafael took in their ancient surroundings beautifully bathed in the bright moonlight.

The next day they were on their way northward to Mexico City. Rafael had packed a large camera for the trip and, upon arriving, began to photograph many of the city's masonry roofs which he had come so far to study, including the celebrated cathedral, one of the largest in the western hemisphere, and many of the city's sixty other churches. He was also interested in the buildings of the University which was founded in 1551, and was flourishing eighty nine years later when Harvard was founded. He was finding that most of the domes in Mexico were built of a single thick shell of brick, sometimes in octagonal form with stone ribs. With his camera's time exposures, the interiors of the buildings were no great problem for him to photograph, but in order to best capture some of the exteriors of these structures, he needed to get permission to go up to the roofs of taller, neighboring buildings. Once atop these roofs, it was sometimes risky moving about trying to find the most advantageous spot from which to aim his camera. Rafael's reports to Elsie of these maneuvers lost nothing in their telling, and Elsie wondered each time he left her for a roof, if she would soon find it necessary to make arrangements to accompany home a box with Rafael in it.

With the best of Mexico City covered, the couple traveled west to Guadalajara to see the city's elaborately decorated cathedral, one of the largest in Mexico, and distinguished by its spires and mix of influences including Baroque, Gothic and Byzantine. For it was begun in 1571 but not completed until more than a century later. Walking from his hotel, Rafael found it standing where four converging plazas came together forming a cross. Spending most of the day studying and photographing the cathedral, he then moved on to the very ornate and beautiful government palace, considered one of the finest examples of Spanish Colonial architecture in Mexico.

Since Rafael and Elsie wanted to return home by train, they planned to enter the United States through El Paso, Texas, and take in the last Mexican city on Rafael's list, San Luis Potosi, which was on the rail line north. Therefore, by a circuitous route east and then north, they headed to this city, founded by a Franciscan monk in 1583, and developed soon after when large gold and silver deposits were discovered. In a short visit, Rafael saw the city's cathedral and government palace. He and Elsie wanted to do a little more touring before heading home, and from El Paso went on north and then west through Arizona to the Grand Canyon. There, Elsie tempted fate by going down into the canyon to the half way point and back on a mule.

By this time it was early April and Elsie was anxious to be on her way home for younger brother Henry's 21st birthday, but Rafael was unsympathetic, wanting to stretch the trip a little further. When Elsie boarded the train and spent the night in the Pullman car, she was expecting to find herself the next day traveling into the Mississippi Valley. But a surprise was in store, for on awakening in the morning, she noticed a wonderful odor which seemed like orange blossoms. Sure enough, on raising the curtain, she was looking out on acres of orange trees covered with beautiful white blossoms. Without her noticing, Rafael had reserved space for them on the train destined for southern California, rather than the one to New York.

Pretty spring flowers, sightseeing, and an excursion to

71

Catalina Island did little to improve Elsie's mood. Tired of traveling and heavy with her confinement now only a few months off, she was relieved when Rafael consented to their heading home in early May. There, she could be reunited with Henry and her friends, and await the arrival of her first child.

NEW YORK

Upon arriving back in New York, Rafael was having some trouble getting back into his work routine. Rather, he wanted to write about his trip, and started putting together his own descriptions of the many cathedrals and palaces in his Mexican photographs. Approaching a well-known trade magazine, he ended up getting the collection published. Then making some more free time, he decided on trying a different kind of construction job. He started building a small observatory inside his home. Buying a refractor-type Clark telescope with a four-inch lens, Rafael chose to mount it not on the flat roof of his house where vibrations from the house or street would be felt, but rather on a cast iron platform mounted on uprights that he built indoors. A movable, circular observatory cover enclosed the telescope. On clear evenings, he delighted in seeing the changing views of the planets and the moon, with eye pieces of 50 to 400 power. And when the weather was clear on weekends, using clouded and angled eye pieces he could view the sun with its changing panorama of spots. Rafael was finally satisfying an interest in astronomy that he'd had since boyhood.

Elsie's baby arrived late in July shortly before expectations, and the story of this sad event is movingly recounted by Elsie's aunt, Florence Anthony. Unable to write to her friend, Helen, Elsie asked her aunt to do so for her. The complete letter follows:

Dear Helen,

I know that you will be as distressed to hear as I am to write you that dear Elsie's little daughter only lived about twelve hours. Elsie had quite a hard time, she was as brave as she could be, but the doctor finally took the baby at about a quarter to eleven on Tuesday. It was quite difficult for the doctor to get the baby to breathe, having to work over it for about three quarters of an hour but at the end of that time he thought it was all right. Only the doctor and nurse were here when the baby came, but when I got here the baby looked too dear for words. It was a perfect little

Acoustictile

baby although it weighed less than six pounds. When we went to bed it seemed to be breathing well and cried lustily but about one o'clock the dear little thing just stopped breathing. Both Elsie and Mr. Guastavino are well nigh broken hearted; but both are brave and Elsie is as near an angel as anyone can be. Elsie says she would appreciate very much your coming and spending next week with her........"

Sincerely,

Florence Currie Anthony

For some time Rafael had been considering building a home out of the city, either for spending the summer or perhaps something year-round. So to get the recent tragedy off Elsie's mind (and his own as well), he took his wife out property hunting in August, as soon as Elsie was feeling a little better. Unlike his father, Rafael was attracted to the water, and seeking the likelihood of cooler summers, the two went out along the south shore of Long Island, taking a room for a few days at a hotel in Long Beach. There, they looked at several good size lots near the ocean. The idea of building a house gave Elsie something to look forward to.

As the fall of 1910 approached, Rafael's thoughts were also on solving a problem that had continually plagued him. It had all started many years ago when he and Blodgett first became aware of all the acoustical problems in buildings where they installed their work. Auditoriums and particularly churches presented the worst sound reverberations, but since the problem had always existed in these buildings, it was not considered a vital matter, and nothing much had been done about it. In auditoriums, felt curtains were sometimes draped across walls to prevent echoes, but no one had found any constructive materials for dealing with the problem. However, about this time, Professor Wallace Sabine at Harvard University was doing important research on the general science of acoustics. Rafael, hearing about Professor Sabine's work and realizing the great need for a building material with sound absorbing qualities approached the Professor who agreed to share his ideas. It was enough to get Rafael started. He headed back to the Company's tile factory in Woburn, Massachusetts and began experiments to develop a sound-absorbing tile.

In the midst of this, Rafael took Elsie to Wilmington, North Carolina where they attended the opening ceremonies of the recently completed St. Mary Church with Guastavino tile ceilings and dome. Then the two went on to Asheville and Black Mountain. Rafael was upset to find that Francesca was still intent on preserving everything just as it was when his father died, just as though he was about to return and all would resume as before. Nor would she consider moving to town for the winter. Rafael left Rhododendron feeling the foreboding of a problem which would grow. Yet that fall he had little time to dwell on it for his Company was working on over a hundred buildings in the East and Midwest. They included a large church in Philadelphia with a 65 foot dome; the State Library and Supreme Court Building in Connecticut; the Chicago and Northwestern Railroad Terminal; and the Vanderbilt Hotel and the lower concourse of Grand Central Station in New York City.

St. Mary Church, Wilmington, North Carolina,
Photo by Frank S. Bua Photography.

76

CHAPTER SIX

EUROPE

Since the trip to Mexico, Rafael had come down with a serious case of wanderlust. Feeling financially secure with so many buildings now under construction, he started thinking about another voyage - this one to Europe. He could tie the trip to business - to his never-ending quest for beautiful, unique tiles that would fit in his specialized tile collection, or be used for upcoming building projects. And while in Europe, he could also look up several long lost relatives. His thoughts wandered ... they could take a side trip to Egypt, a country he'd always wanted to explore. And to add to the excitement, he and Elsie would return home on the much anticipated maiden voyage of the ship, "Titanic." Elsie was receptive to the whole idea. And Rafael started plans for a very ambitious itinerary. They would need to leave before Christmas so as to return in time for spring building projects. The prospect of spending the holidays away from Henry and friends was somewhat upsetting to Elsie, but when Rafael suggested celebrating Christmas in Paris, she came around to his thinking.

In mid December, they embarked on the White Star liner "Oceanic" for Cherbourg, with plans after Paris of spending four months visiting Egypt, Italy and Spain. Elsie kept a complete diary on the trip. While some of what she wrote could be considered rather tedious, there remain some letters to her friend Helen which are quite the opposite.

Elsie wrote her friend on the train from Cherbourg to Paris:

The train is made up of amusing little compartments like stage scenery. On the walls are pictures together with a mirror and a map of France. We are passing through quaint old Normandy. I think of you as you said you would love so to see this country and the habits of the people over here. Although it is only two days before Christmas, the gardens are green as well as the grass, making the whole country look a fresh green. All along there are picturesque stone houses with blue slate, red tile or thatched moss-grown roofs in towns with the spire of a church or a cathedral in the midst. There are funny old peasant women in their starched white caps with kerchiefs, and men in sort of Turkish bloomer type trousers of corduroy, some with fur coats which seem unnecessary. There are stylishly dressed people to be seen, too. The country just now is flooded with overflowing brooks. I've seen some pretty walled in gardens, and on the farms there are many big red and white cows....

The next letter was written on Christmas Day:

Hotel Meurice
Rue de Rivoli
Paris
Xmas

Dear Helen,

We are having the time of our lives – just enjoying ourselves in the most perfect hotel you could ever imagine. Paris to me is just like a dream city, it is so full of beautiful buildings, parks, boulevards and sculpture. It is a little difficult to become accustomed to the profuse display of undraped female figures - statuary in the parks and on monuments, that is, but I have succeeded and now admire them very much. You can't imagine what a joy it is to me to see in a city, beauty wherever you turn. I just said today I'd like to stay here the rest of my life.

I wish you were along with us autoing about to see the life of the streets – singers, violinists and acrobats performing on the pavement. I'd like to go on a lot more but we are going to hear "Faust" at the Grand Opera House tonight and I have to dress now. Please write.....

Under the diary date of December 28, there appears the

following foreboding entry.

Among other errands, we have engaged passage home on the maiden trip of the SS Titanic for May 1.

That December night they entrained for Marseilles where they would board the "SS China" for Port Said. Elsie had enjoyed Marseilles and was particularly impressed with the donkeys pulling carts, and performing dogs and acrobats on the dock.

On January 2, the two arrived in Port Said and were met at the dock by Mohamed Rashdan who was to be their personal guide.

The next letter to Helen is from Egypt:

Mena House Hotel
Pyramids, Cairo
January 5, 1912

Dear Helen,

....you can see from this paper where we are; the Sphinx is here too but the size is very disappointing in comparison to the Pyramids.

We left Cairo about 9 this morning accompanied by our guide Mohamed Rashdan (I will send you his picture and others taken today very soon) and after an interesting train ride watching the people going to the city with their wares laden on camels and donkeys we arrived here about 10:30. We walked up to the Pyramids and then each of us took 3 Arab men (hired by Rashdan with much squabbling) to get us to the top. The pyramid is 470 feet high and the stones of which it is made by which you can climb are three to four feet high. The ascent is very steep so a man takes each a hand and one boosts from behind going up. Coming down, the booster holds onto you by a string around your waist. I was supposed to go only half way up but once that far Rafael said "Come on," so on I went and was glad of it although I was

79

Men playing chess in Egypt.
Photo by Rafael Guastavino III.

already very worried about managing the descent when I looked back. Although we rushed the whole time up the tremendous stones, the last half seemed shorter than the first half. When we reached the top there was a sort of celebration with the Arabs up there who served us hot coffee "a la Turque." We had perfectly glorious views of the desert on one side, with the town, palm trees and fertile green valley of the Nile on the other side. We could see the citadel of Cairo and the whole view had a beautiful soft yellowish pink sky in the background. It was one of the most beautiful sights I have ever seen, certainly in the most interesting circumstances possible. As additional local color, one of the Arabs was playing native music on a kind of flute with the rest clapping and gibbering Arabic trying to persuade one of their number to dance.

Interesting conversation followed as most of them spoke English. It makes me disgusted with myself for not being able to speak a foreign language. I was as pleasant as I knew how to be as you feel entirely in their hands and at their mercy if they got disagreeable. Some of them had two wives each and seemed to know all about our system of only having one. I don't think they understood me when I said, "Anyway, we only have one at a time." They seemed very well satisfied with their way.

Well, I better hurry on! After lunch at this very nice hotel, we took camels and rode all around the three pyramids and the Sphinx. I can say that camel riding is great although I feel my writing is shaky after my first ride on one. When the creature gets up and down you have to go through quite a performance of leaning first way back and then way forward in accordance with his gentle but extreme motions. Of course, getting down is the other way around. We got on and off several times so I feel quite expert now. When riding at a walk you have to relax and just sway around in time with the creature's steps which are rather queer. But when they trot on the soft sand it is really very comfortable and nice. It was great fun; my camel man sang weird Arabic songs and the lovely strange scenery was so enjoyable. I had a nice young camel that didn't make awful groaning noises when it got up and down as the old ones do.

81

Under the date of January 12, Elsie wrote in her diary:

While I was packing for the trip up the Nile and writing cards, Rafael was at the bazaars with Rashdan where he had a tremendous row about tiles he was buying. Everyone was talking a different language and police were watching. In the end Rafael won out. In the afternoon we drove to several mosques and tombs on the outskirts of the city.

On January 13, they left Cairo and Rashdan for a trip up the Nile by river steamer "Rameses." As day followed day, the notation Elsie wrote under "weather" became a monotonous "perfect." The air was cool and dry but hot in the sun. Living on the steamer which was comfortable and sparsely occupied, they soon became very friendly with some of their fellow passengers. Before the trip was over, Rafael had found several fellow chess players with whom to test his skill, and Elsie reported that on one occasion he also found a congenial audience to lecture to on astronomy.

The steamer took them to Thebes, Karnak, Luxor, Aswan, Philae, and other ancient occupied places and temples less well-known. Elsie noted in her diary thoughts about the villages – the people, water wheels, animals. As the steamer docked or anchored, the excursion party would go ashore, by ferry if necessary. Then all would all ride donkeys to the ancient remains.

In Egypt, Rafael was finding success in buying the antique, glazed tiles he was seeking for several jobs and for his Mediterranean tile collection. While in Cairo, he needed to spend almost an entire day negotiating between a dealer and the American consul who made all the necessary arrangements for his newly purchased tiles to be shipped back to New York. Then, each tile had to be carefully packed so as not to break in transit.

The trip continued by boat - past Sicily.

"We have passed Messina which was so wrecked by the earth-

quake," writes Elsie. " Mt. Etna is hidden with clouds but we see Stromboli, the big mountain rising straight from the sea ....We could see people with glasses and noticed the crooked condition of the earth due to earthquakes."

February 1: Welcome Italy! Wonderful, wonderful day. Had a grand view of Vesuvius just before and after a sunrise. As a beautiful background, there was the exquisite scenery of the Bay of Naples ....the life and street scenes are more picturesque than I imagined ....some streets are just narrow steps down and each time there is a glimpse of the bay, it makes a lovely picture. There are walled vineyards and orange groves with snow-capped mountains in the distance. At our Grand Hotel we have a delightful evening's entertainment by Neapolitans in native costume playing string instruments, singing and dancing, incidently taking collections...

From Naples to Pompeii, Amalfi, then Sorrento and Capri.

February 6, Sorrento and Capri: ...rough sea on the way to Capri but didn't get sick. The water was a deep blue and the mountainous shore rising straight from the water, a lovely soft velvety brown. We embarked in small boats to the Blue Grotto and lying flat swished through the little entrance in a furious rush. Inside the limpid blue water of a different shade, brightly reflected on the cave ceiling overhead was a glorious sight. Rough run back to Naples and this time was sick...

Four nights later, they boarded an overnight steamer to Palermo, Sicily.

February 10, visiting Girgenti: ...the Temples, which are ideally picturesque, the simple beauty of the ancient Greek architecture set in such a perfect combination of mountains and sea.

February 12, Taormina : ..... went up to the Teatro Greco:

83

the remains of an ancient Greek amphitheater, in itself an interesting old ruin. But from almost any spot in the whole place you get a gorgeous view of smoking snow-clad Mt. Etna: the flower-decked countryside dotted with towns and houses, and the attractive outline of the sea with its brilliant coloring. The straights of Messina and the shore of Italy are in the distance...

On February 21, they arrived in Rome.

To see Rome in limited time is the biggest proposition in the world. We are five days behind schedule and anxious to catch up but there is so much to see and we would hate to miss anything important...... talk about studying at school, it isn't anything to seeing and remembering the art treasures here. It is delightful to see the originals of the pictures in my school books ....You must come to Rome some day if you never go anywhere else; it's the greatest treat in the world....

From Rome the journey continued. And Elsie kept writing.

Pisa – .... to cathedral which with Baptistry and Campanile, the famous leaning tower, make a beautiful group. The tower leaning terrifically makes a strange sight. We spent a strenuous morning climbing to the top and enjoyed the lovely panorama of the city, countryside and surrounding mountains with the river Arno flowing through. It is very scary standing on the higher balconies!

On March 5, Elsie wrote Helen from Venice.

Venice is fascinating. I never imagined it would be quite as quaint and charming as it is. The gondolas on the canals are such fun and the old palaces very beautiful. The smart private gondolas and classy little motor boats fitted up just like automobiles are very interesting to watch. We'll never forget arriving at the hotel by moonlight in a gondola.

We have enjoyed St. Mark's, the square, the Piazzetta, and the Doges Palace so much. The pigeons are the dearest things and so tame. Of course, I'll have a picture of myself feeding them. Rafael says it's a shame to feed them because everyone does and they are so fat.

We are both crazy about the Venetian lace but the prices are awful. We have a few nice pieces and now Rafael is concerned about the additional high duties he will have to pay when we return home."

Rafael appended a note to this letter as follows:

At every stop we make, Elsie says, 'it's the greatest ever.' After Paris, it was Cairo, then Naples - which nothing could surpass - followed by Vesuvius, Pompeii, Capri. Of course, Rome took the prize, and now none can compare to Venice. I think she is dreaming so I pinch her every now and then to see if she is really awake. In her diary, you will find three or four words on every line like these: Wonderful, grand, loveliest, charming, fascinating, elegant, marvelous, tremendous, colossal, greatest, most beautiful, etc., etc. She might as well get a rubber stamp and put them in that way to save time.

After a side trip to the lake country north of Milan, they went on to the Riviera and to Monte Carlo, where at the casino Rafael tried a system of betting on red or black to come up inconsistently. Amidst a lot of cheering and encouragement from Elsie, he won ten dollars. Returning the next night, he told Elsie that he would give her all his winnings. Elsie writes: *I started building great air castles – one vision was to give Henry a dress suit he needs for his birthday, but then – pouff ! With the doubling up, Rafael suddenly lost $31 and we were so disgusted –Boo-ho. But the various characters at the tables were very amusing.*

They left on March 19 for Spain arriving in Barcelona two days later after stops at Nice and Cannes. Elsie wrote: *...thrilled to be in my dearie's native land and we are both so pleased to be here together and see the house where he was born.*

On the afternoon of the 25th, they took the train to

Elliptic dome in Valencia

Valencia and were met at the station by a brother of Rafael Sr.,
Tio Pepe, and a cousin, Maria Louisa, who spoke English to
Elsie's pleasant surprise. They all went together to the Grand
Hotel and had tea. In the evening, Tio Pepe brought two other
relatives to call and Elsie was sorry not to be able to speak
Spanish with them. One was Vincenti Guastavino, a lawyer, and
the other, a cousin, Carlotta.

Their goal the following day was to see two buildings
which Rafael Sr. had used as models for buildings he later
designed in the United States. It was partly the success of these
buildings that aroused his interest in emigrating to America. One
was formerly used as a silk exchange and had inspired his
Spanish Building at the Chicago World's Fair. The other was the
"Coppella de los Desamparados," the elliptical dome that
influenced his designs for St Lawrence Church in Asheville.

Making two short side trips by rail from Valencia, they
visited Segundo and saw remains of a Roman amphitheater and
forts built by the Moors. In the afternoon after a lunch of
"Paella," the locally featured dish of rice with seafood, they
jumped on the train heading for the small town of Segorge, in
order to meet another brother of Rafael Sr. - Tio Antonio. From
Elsie's enthusiastic description, personality in Rafael Sr.'s
generation must have reached some kind of peak in Tio Antonio.
He was the widower who in later life became a Franciscan monk
and was living in a monastery nearby. Elsie wrote,

*We first saw him running up the station platform in his
brown robes waving a handkerchief with both hands. He has the
most beautiful face of any old man in the world, especially when
he smiles. He had planned a delightful little excursion through
the country along a river and he was so happy to have us with
him. He is young in enthusiasm and walked so energetically as
though he was a boy. I fell in love with him immediately and I'm
glad he loves me too. He returned with us to Valencia and we all
had dinner with Tio Pepe.*

The next day they saw Tio Antonio again and before he

left Valencia he gave each a blest crucifix and a medal. "I felt badly at leaving him so soon," wrote Elsie. "I grew up to love him so much I couldn't help crying when we kissed each other goodbye. I hope I see him again before he dies."

Before leaving Valencia, Rafael and Elsie visited several tile factories, and at one were treated to an elaborate luncheon at the home of the factory owner. Paella was again the "piece de resistance," this time the large circular dish was placed for serving in a wreath of flowers. Tio Pepe held a farewell champagne dinner for them on the evening of the 29th of March at which gifts were exchanged, and Carlotta entertained by playing the piano. The next morning they left for Madrid where Elsie would write Helen about meeting and falling in love with Rafael's family. In Madrid, Rafael would buy over a hundred tiles for his collection. It is here that Elsie hints at being a little homesick. But not until a few days later when they stop in Granada is she outwardly tiring of the trip. "The people here are very rude to tourists," she writes in her diary, "this especially applies to the native girls; one young beauty stuck her tongue out at me."

The next letter comes from Sevilla on April 13, 1912.

Dear Helen,

It's a sure thing that enough is a plenty, or some such saying, for example on the first part of the trip I considered dreams about being home again a nightmare, but now I'm looking forward to getting home like going to paradise. When I'm on the go and seeing the beautiful and interesting things here and I am still delighted but as soon as a lull in the program comes I'm like a hen on a hot griddle. Our funds are becoming a little limited so we seem to be loafing along to take up the time now.

Rafael is making a splendid collection of tiles, and I am hoping that it will prove to be practical on account of speaking the language like a native he makes wonderful bargains with the antique dealers. I stay in the hotel so as not to give him away because although it seems to me that I look quite like some Spanish girls who wear hats (mantillas are usually worn) I always seem to be spotted.

...When we get home, we plan to go to Bay Shore just as soon as possible so as not to have to open up the Green Avenue house. As you know, we expect to arrive on the 6th. We were booked for the maiden trip of the Titanic but we see by the Paris edition of the New York Herald of April 10 (just received) that she made her maiden trip earlier than expected and is already at sea. However since her schedule calls for her to return in time we will expect to depart on her as planned from Cherbourg. Watch the papers for our arrival time and if it is at a civilized hour please come to meet us. I'm just crazy to see you again and if I'm not sufficient attraction the largest ship afloat will be a great treat to see. A quote from the Herald, "The passenger on the Titanic may keep himself fit by exercise in the gymnasium or by a game in the squash racquets court, proceed to the Turkish, electric or swimming baths and then finish with a two mile stroll on the spacious decks." Some class! It's just as well we are missing the maiden voyage because the special tips expected would have busted us entirely. As it is, I will arrive looking like a tramp as I am seeing my spring Paris outfit fade in the distance with our diminishing funds.

It is dinner time so I have to close. Hasta Manana (until tomorrow) or in other words until the longed for 6th of May.
—Very lovingly, E.

In the diary under April 18:

.....Had light lunch and walked to depot to take train to Madrid. We got settled in our compartment and Rafael bought a Spanish newspaper. It was then that we had one of the greatest shocks of our lives to learn that the Titanic had run into an iceberg and sunk with a horrible loss of life. We felt so badly we could hardly believe it to be true. The trip to Madrid seemed years long and we went right to Cooks and heard definitely the terrible news. At the

hotel we got a Herald and spent the evening reading all the news possible from it about the loss of the poor Titanic, the greatest of modern tragedies.

The next day they were offered space on the "Olympic" sailing on the 24th, and they accepted it. After a stop-over at Burgos, they arrived in Paris on the 22nd, but of the rest of the trip there is little to relate, since the daily entries in the diary nearly cease. What is known is that they sailed home on the 26th not on the Olympic as planned, but went to Le Havre and boarded "La Provence." The ship docked in New York on May 4th, and there are these words: "Home – Hip! Hip! Hooray!" And Elsie had something else to cheer about for she had recently become aware that she was expecting another child in December.

CHAPTER SEVEN

BAY SHORE

It was the summer of 1912. Rafael and Elsie were spending most of their free time on Long Island aboard their new 36 foot cabin cruiser, "Don Quixote," which Rafael had named after the celebrated character created by Spanish novelist, Cervantes. One breezy afternoon, they boarded the boat for a trip across Great South Bay to Fire Island, and as usual took along crew, Tommy Thompson, who would tend to all the lines and help with docking and mooring. On this day he would also add a little excitement to their excursion.

Enjoying a morning of sunshine and sightseeing, Rafael decided to drop anchor in the shallow waters off Fire Island, and set up for lunch. As he and Elsie sat watching a school of fish feeding nearby, Tommy climbed up the boat's mast to get a better view. All was peaceful when suddenly there was a scream and great thud. Tommy losing his grip on the wooden mast, had come hurtling down landing in a heap on the cabin top. Momentarily stunned, he took a few seconds to peel himself off the wood. The young boy, dressed in his blue sailor's uniform, apologized profusely to Rafael, who having taken a liking to his young crew, requested that he limit his mast climbing in the future.

The cottage they rented that summer on Bay Shore was comfortable and convenient, yet Rafael was ready now to build his own place on Long Island. Elsie would be having the baby in a few months and they would want a spot to call home. By this time, he had definite ideas about the house, and decided to ask his architect friend, Henry Hornbostel, to work with him. The house he desired would naturally show some Spanish qualities, and be built principally of masonry with cohesive tile construction. On his trip to Europe, Rafael had studied the designs of many different buildings which in one way or another might be used as examples in designing his own house. Therefore, in searching for a site to build on, he kept in mind the type of house so that site and building would be compatible. Since he wanted navigable water-front for the boat, this narrowed his choices. What caught his eye was a 30 acre water-front lot which was marshy and being developed by a wealthy sugar producer from New York City. The businessman owned most of the point and land to the main road through the south shore. He had built for himself a large summer house of 25 rooms on an expansive lot half way from the main road to the point; then realized that the area should grow with the increase of wealthy commuters. So he filled in the marsh and offered large lots on it for sale. As the asking price was reasonable, Rafael bought two large water-front lots comprising a little over two acres of bulk-headed filled-in land. Looking south from the water's edge, one could see Fire Island a few miles away.

After arranging for a future summer lease for their cottage, Rafael and Elsie returned to their Green Avenue, Brooklyn home for the winter, he with the project of drawing up the plans for their new house, and she to await the expected arrival in December. In due time this took place successfully on December 17; the baby was a boy, and the name chosen for him was Rafael (IV).

As time permitted, the company draftsman worked on the house plans, with Rafael overseeing the style and general layout. In March of 1913, ground was broken. The foundations for a heavy masonry house to be built on filled-in land posed the first serious problem. All masonry work has a strong tendency to crack because of the shrinkage of cement as it hardens, and when insecure foundations are added, the resulting cracks increase in size and number. In this case, the problem was solved largely by springing the interior cohesive arches from deep piers, and raising the outside walls of the house from extra heavy concrete footings well reinforced. Since these footings were continuous around the house, they tended to make the whole outside structure monolithic, but the interior piers for the arches were the real problem. Workers dug down through the fill, then through the mud of the old marsh until many feet further down they finally reached a bed of gravel upon which to start building them. Then as walls and piers were raised high enough, arches were built from pier to pier and the sides of the arches filled to provide level spring lines for barrel vaults between the arches. The general design of the house gave it a boxlike appearance except from the northwest where it was irregularly indented. Above the ceilings of the first floor, however, the construction was much more conventional.

The plan for Rafael's Spanish style home called for a pitched roof of corrogated red tile, and a tower which Elsie particularly wanted. Then, a third floor tower room was added to the design where Rafael would have his studio. There he could display the tiles and other art objects he'd collected in Europe. From the studio, a door led into the attic where two tall windows set side by side provided most of the light. With a column and two small Moorish arches, the house took on an even more Spanish flavor.

By May, Rafael, Elsie and the baby moved out of the city and into a rental cottage at Bay Shore. Rafael had been thinking about driving for some time. A friend of his owned a small car (appropriately called a "Little") which he wanted to sell in order to buy a larger one. So Rafael bought the little car and, and his friend taught him how to drive it. Already in his forties, Rafael didn't take easily to handling a car, and over the years only his cautious ways kept him out of serious trouble. Nevertheless, he was always very free with advice to anyone else who might happen to be at the wheel of a car in which he was riding. The younger and more adaptable Elsie, however, took to the road as one in her own element, and became the principal chauffeur of the family, driving every day to the work site.

Building continued through the summer on the 3- story house; the pitched roof of Spanish tile, the many columns and archways, and third floor tower were slowly taking shape. However, work on the walls of the house was stalled. Rafael's long experience in building had conditioned him to anticipate and avoid any flaw in building plans which would result in leaks. Yet, with his own house he made one of his most regrettable errors. He chose not ordinary brick for his house walls, but a square hollow

"Tile House" Bay Shore, Long Island,
R.J. Guastavino Collection.

red brick, not realizing that in addition to its being hollow, the material was more porous than ordinary brick. Elsie disliked Rafael's selection from the beginning because of its square appearance. She preferred the ordinary rectangular brick.

The building of the house was attracting considerable attention in Bay Shore, particularly among family and friends. Sightseers were frequent visitors, too, initially to see the unique construction of the lower floor. Later on, they were surprised by the unusual height of the house. As the builders reached the roofing stage, Henry and his friends would climb the scaffolding and rave about the spectacular view.

By early December, the Bay Shore house was finished enough so that Rafael could move his family in, so young Rafael's first birthday and Christmas were celebrated there. But in the first month of 1914, Rafael's excitement in his new home was overshadowed by the mistake that he'd made. The use of the odd-shaped hollow brick for his walls was proving a disaster. In mid-December there were several heavy rain storms with strong winds from the east beating on the high facade of the house. The twenty and thirty mile an hour winds forced rain through the porous material and the water trickled down the hollow spaces in the walls, accumulating as it descended. Around the first floor windows and doors, it seemed like a flood was coming in. A northeast wind with rain is never welcomed during the winter by anyone; but Rafael dreaded seeing the wind shift that way, for when it did, pans, towels, and mops were hauled out to stem the tide. Indeed, he soon found that rain from any direction tended to seep through the walls when driven by a high wind. Before March was over, all the wall-papered walls on the east side of the house and the plaster ceilings near them were water stained. In an effort to close the pores of the house walls, Rafael found some paint-like products on the market that would, for the time being, prevent the worst of the leaking. So in the spring, he had the walls of the house "water-proofed." This worked reasonably well, and with the thought that with several more applications over the next year or so he could solve the worst of the problem, his mood improved. Both he and Elsie were also cheered by the knowledge that she was expecting another child in the fall.

Rafael continued working on his new prized possession with the next project being a cement pond built between the house and the water. Then, in the center of the lawn beside the house, a clay tennis court was laid out with high wire netting at each end. Elsie and particularly Rafael loved showing off their property and new home, and invited many friends to come visit. Arriving callers would first have to climb a half dozen brick steps, since the house was set high to take full advantage of the water view to the east and south. Through a massive front door, they would enter the front hall which possessed a tile ceiling with an archway spanning about twelve feet. Then to the right and up a few steps through a pair of carved wooden doors, they would enter a large living room. Here, the walls were paneled with cypress; the flat ceiling consisted of dark blue glazed tile laid without mortar between narrowly spaced wooden beams. In the center of the room's south wall was a large fireplace with two inlaid marble columns and a high overhanging tile mantle near the ceiling. The adjoining porch was all glass. The house with its beautiful tiled archways and ceilings was considered magnificent for its day, but Rafael's dining room was the "piece de resistance." Looking through its large window, one could enjoy a panoramic view of the water. For those dining, it felt as if they were eating outdoors.

In August, the Blodgetts came to visit and see Rafael's creation, but their stay was overshadowed by the momentous events in Europe where war had broken out. Since both families had traveled extensively on the Continent, they identified with the regions under siege, and were appalled by the desecration of Belgium. Rafael and Blodgett would stay up into the early morning hours talking about the uncertain future of Europe.

Yet, there was some good news that year, for on November 21, Elsie gave birth to a daughter who was named Louise.

Under Professor Sabine's guidance, Rafael was spending more time working at the Company's tile factory in Woburn, trying to discover a highly porous but strong ceramic material that could absorb and quell sound waves. His first solution was to thoroughly mix short fibered peat into high quality clay. After molding this mixture into the shape of a tile, it was burned in the kiln and thus hardened into a strong ceramic material. With the peat burned out, it was left honey-combed with holes. This invention was patented with the name "Rumford" in honor of Count Rumford, a prominent early American scientist born in Woburn who would become an international figure in the late eighteenth century. Rafael's new tile became immediately popular, and orders started coming in, first from the churches of St. Vincent Ferrer and St. Thomas in New York City. Rafael was bolstered by the fact that he'd developed the first acoustic tile for manufacture, but he soon realized that while Rumford tile was a tremendous step forward in the conquest of echoes, reverberations, and general noise in public buildings, it was still not ideal. For one thing, the burning and mixing processes were very costly. And for another, in spite of the extensive mixing, the peat could not be made to evenly spread through the tile. Where the peat was overly concentrated, the tile was weak, and it took very little stress in handling to break it. Also, the pores of the tile tended to fill with dust, and cleaning it was next to impossible.

So into 1915, Rafael continued his search for something more effective, and possibly lighter and cheaper to manufacture. It occurred to him that another way for a material to be porous was if it was made of small round objects glued together. But what would it be made of, and how could it be fastened together? The two questions consumed him. Tiny grains of sand, he thought, were too smooth to be held together with a coating of cement, and would also make too heavy a tile. Then his thoughts turned to the light, porous volcanic rock, pumice, for pumice was available in granular form and could be graded into different sized granules from fine to very coarse. Working day and night for months, Rafael experimented with what became the ultimate in truly acoustic masonry. Thoroughly mixing the granules of pumice with wet cement, the cement would coat each particle of pumice. Then the mixture was placed under a hand-operated

Church of St. Vincent Ferrer, New York City.
From R. Guastavino Co. Catalogue.

press in the size of a desired tile. After a given amount of pressure from the press, the "green" tile was removed from the form and placed aside for the cement to dry. Wherever the particles of pumice touched one another, the hardened cement strongly held them together. By using different size particles, the sound absorbing character of the tile could be altered for higher pitched sounds or lower ones, such as organ music in cathedrals. This new tile, named "Akoustolith," encompassed all the improvements Rafael had strived for. The first patent was granted about a year later, with Professor Sabine named as co-inventor.

Magnified photograph of Akoustolith material showing porosity.

By 1917, the Guastavino Company was ready to exploit great opportunities with the development of Akoustolith tile, but war involvement put a tight damper on public building construction, particularly the type where tile ceiling construction might be used. While architects were showing considerable interest in the new tile, their plans to use it largely had to be put on hold. Rafael suddenly found a lot of time on his hands, as there was little to do at the office, so he took on a new project. He rigged up a pottery turntable and a kerosene kiln in the shop room of his garage and began turning out some ordinary burned clay pieces; then he began experimenting with glazes. Eventually, he made some imitation antique Persian glazed tiles which were so fine that they were exhibited some years later in a show at the Metropolitan Museum of Art in New York. Some of his luster glazes were also included in the show.

With their Akoustolith patent secure and with the accumulated back log of war postponed building projects, Rafael and the Guastavino Company had every reason to believe that new monumental building prospects would continue to develop. And, indeed, what would become one of his greatest masterpieces appeared on the horizon.

For some time, Rafael had been working on plans for extensive work in the new Nebraska State Capitol building at Lincoln. The building was designed by architect, Bertram Goodhue, who had used Rumford tile in his designs for St. Thomas and St. Vincent Ferrer churches in New York. Of all the large works ever done by the Guastavino Company, this one would use most extensively its unique combination of crafts. First, was the self-supporting tile masonry vaulting, and with that the use of the sound-absorbing Akoustolith tile. Also, Hildreth Meiere, a prominent mural artist, designed extensive decorative work for the Capitol, including large figures and lettering to be done in colors with glazed tile set in a mosaic with the Akoustolith.

The Nebraska State Capitol job would become a painstaking challenge for Rafael for in producing finished glazed tiles for the murals, many steps were involved. The first was to break up the full size color drawings into tile size pieces with each piece assigned its own color - there were 14 colors in all. Many mixtures of suitable chemicals were made up to produce the desired color samples and then they were fired in the kiln at the factory. When enough samples were finished, they were shown to Hildreth Meiere. The colors chosen for each piece were then set up for duplication on tile biscuits of the right shape to make up the decorative forms.

In theory, all this was not particularly difficult to work out, but the problem of duplicating the desired glazes was nearly impossible. If the quantity of the chemicals was correct, the quality of the chemicals sometimes varied, and so the resulting color after firing did also. But the firing was the most difficult variable to control, for heat and particularly the time of the glaze in the heat had to be exactly duplicated, too. Hildreth Meiere was a perfectionist and rejected many tiles so the manufacture of many extra batches of tiles became a necessity. During the preparation and manufacture of all the glazed tiles, Rafael was at the factory taking charge from breaking down the original drawings to the final firing of the kiln.*

The Nebraska State Capitol was the country's first vernacular Capitol - differing dramatically from the architecture of traditional State Capitols. The building features a low square foundation of floors with a 400 foot tower rising upward from the center. Atop the tower is a dome. The whole structure resembles a cross and soon took on the nickname "Cathedral of the Prairie." An architectural masterpiece, it took 10 years and nearly 10 million dollars to build, and was a hugely successful project for the R. Guastavino Company entering the 1930's.

* A lesser example of this type of work was installed by the Company in the ceiling of the crypt of the National Shrine at Catholic University in Washington, D.C.

Nebraska State Capitol, interior view,
From R. Guastavino Company Catalogue.

Nebraska State Capitol seen from the northwest.
Photographed by Sid Spelts, 1991.
Image courtesy of the Nebraska Capitol Collections.

End of Book I

POST SCRIPT

NOTABLE DEVELOPMENTS

"Whispering Corners"

Witness an acoustical masterpiece of Guastavino architecture. Located outside The Oyster Bar in Grand Central Station is a small tile archway where two people can stand diagonally across from one another (about 30 feet apart), whisper into the corner of the wall, and be heard as if speaking face to face. A popular spot on Valentine's Day, many marriage proposals have reportedly been made at "whispering corners."

Whispering Corners,
Photo courtesy of Mary S. Saner

How does it work? Sound travels along the curve of the arch - a trait of many Guastavino ceilings including those of The Oyster Bar itself.

Dining room, Courtesy of
The Grand Central Oyster Bar & Restaurant in New York City.

105

"Seven To Save"

When word spread that the Guastavino Bay Shore, Long Island home built in 1913 was on the market, and that a potential buyer was considering demolition, a group of historical preservationists rallied to save it. The Preservation League of New York state chose the "Tile House" as one of New York's "Seven To Save."

Registry Room at Ellis Island

It took 28,832 tiles for the Guastavinos to rebuild the ceiling in the Great Hall at Ellis Island after the "Black Tom Explosion" of 1918. As a result of the perfected vaulting technique and the endurance of the strong, lightweight, fireproof tiles, only 17 new tiles were needed for the renovation in the 1980's sponsored by the Statue of Liberty/Ellis Island Foundation.

Guastavino's

Underneath the Queensboro Bridge in New York City is the eclectic restaurant, Guastavino's, named in honor of the signature architecture surrounding it. The herringbone patterned vaulting in two kiosks and in the tile archway below the Bridge give a distinct Guastavino flavor to the area.

Guastavino's
Courtesy of Guastavino's, Inc.,
New York City

Biltmore Estate

George W. Vanderbilt's home in Asheville is now surrounded by a hotel and a winery and is known as the Biltmore Estate. Having 34 bedrooms, 43 baths and 65 fireplaces, "America's largest home" also houses a hugely valuable collection of art and antiques.

The author, Rafael Guastavino IV

ABOUT THE AUTHOR

Rafael Guastavino IV, now 93, came to the Eastern Shore of Maryland from Bay Shore, Long Island in the early 1940's. A good friend had recently moved to a house on Worton Creek and invited him to come down and look around the Tidewater area. After exploring Cambridge and Salisbury, he visited Kent County and decided to stay awhile in Chestertown's Old Bell Haven, then a restaurant and boarding house, now Washington College's Literary House. Soon he was making friends with the many professors who'd cross the street to have some tea or a meal.

Taking a liking to the people, climate and way of life on the Eastern Shore, Mr. Guastavino bought a small farm outside Fairlee. Nicknamed by the locals, "Starve and Go Naked," it was considered poor farmland, but the county agricultural agent recommended covering the property with loblolly pines for timber and to improve the soil. Soon after, the author tried beekeeping here which began as a hobby, but blossomed into a profitable business. A few years later, taking a job with a federal ag group doing farm surveys, he discovered Island Point Farm in Rock Hall with its 93 acres of fields, woods and shoreline along Langford Creek's West Fork. It was here he would settle (now almost 60 years) and grow corn, soybeans and wheat, as well as raise Holstein cows.

An avid hunter, Mr. Guastavino shot dove and ducks on his property for many years, and now leases parts of his farm to hunters in the fall and spring. Also a sailor, he raced Stars as a child in the shallow waters of Great South Bay near Fire Island; then, after moving to Maryland, bought a Comet and Sunfish to use with his own children on Langford Bay and the Chester River.

Over time, Mr. Guastavino acquired a knack for investing in the stock market. Working for free as a financial advisor to the Chestertown Library, he, for years, made decisions on how library funds would be invested. He still follows the stock market on a daily basis.

Mr. Guastavino wrote this book to tell the story of his family. At one time, he, like his father and grandfather, wanted to be an architect, attending the University of Miami School of Architecture for a year before it closed due to lack of funds (it reopened in 1983). But after a long stint of poor health, he gave up school. Thereafter, his father discouraged him from working in the family's company for lack of an architectural degree. Yet luckily, he says, he found the Eastern Shore - for farming, sailing, hunting and the simplicity of rural life has suited him just fine.

He and his wife, Helen, have three children.

George R. Collins (now deceased) was formerly Professor of Art History at Columbia University.

ACKNOWLEDGMENTS

I am very grateful to my wife, Helen, who so diligently typed my early manuscript, and to Mary Saner, editor, agent and good friend.